Restored to Sanity

Essays on the Twelve Steps
by Unitarian Universalists

Edited by Ken and Cathlean

D1600404

Skinner House Books
Boston

Published by Skinner House Books, an imprint of the Unitarian Universalist Association, a liberal religious organization with more than 1,000 congregations in the U.S. and Canada, 24 Farnsworth St., Boston, MA 02210–1409.

www.skinnerhouse.org

Printed in the United States

Cover design by Kathryn Sky-Peck
Text design by Suzanne Morgan

print ISBN: 978-1-55896-742-7
eBook ISBN: 978-1-55896-743-4

6 5 4 3 2 1
17 16 15 14

We gratefully acknowledge permission to reprint "If I Did Not Pray" by Rabia of Basra, translated by Daniel Ladinsky, in *Love Poems from God: Twelve Sacred Voices from the East and West*, published by the Penguin Group, Inc., copyright © 2002 by Daniel Ladinsky. Reprinted by permission of translator.

Contents

Introduction

This book is not just about the Twelve Steps. It is a direct result of the work that the Twelve Steps invite us to do as people in recovery if we want to live happier, healthier, and more whole lives. Sometimes this work is incredibly painful. Sometimes it is a great blessing. Often, it is both.

Ken: On the morning of September 19, 2005, I had a meeting with my co-editor, Cathlean. She had come to my office to interview me for another book she was writing at the time. As she entered the room, I waved but didn't extend my hand in greeting. Instead, I said that I had caught some sort of bug and was feeling sick. Out of concern for her well-being, I'd be sitting far away from her, not wanting to share the illness. That was a lie.

I was hungover. I was sure I stunk of booze. I felt as if I might be sick at any moment. I was physically and emotionally unsteady.

It was also one of the most important days of my life. September 19, 2005, was the first day of the continuous sobriety that I have maintained to this day and will maintain for the rest of my life—God willing, and with the help of the Twelve Steps and people who have committed to working with them. Of course, at the time that Cathlean and I met, I didn't know any of what would come to be. I only knew that I was feeling the same dread, pain, and anxiety I had experienced countless times before, but that this time, something had to change. I had no idea how that would happen. So I lied to Cathlean out of my fear and shame.

A couple years later, I ran into her at General Assembly, the annual gathering of Unitarian Universalists, as I had hoped I someday would. I asked if she and I might find a quiet space together to talk. When we sequestered ourselves, I took a deep breath and said, "I have something to tell you, an apology that's important for me to offer to you. That day when we met in my office a couple years ago? I lied to you. I had a hangover. I was ashamed to honestly admit what was really going on with me, and so I lied to you. I am sorry."

I went on to offer a few more details about that day and what had happened in my life since. She listened calmly, intently. I concluded, hoping that she might be able to forgive me, but I had no expectation that she would. I thanked her for giving me this space and her time.

She smiled at me. "You know what?" she replied, "I've got something to share with you as well."

I was amazed by and grateful for what I heard. . . .

Cathlean: When I walked into Ken's office that morning, I remember thinking to myself, "Wow, he is really sick! I hope I don't get what he's got!" The truth of the matter was, of course, that in fact I had. We both share the disease of alcoholism.

What Ken didn't know on the day of our meeting was that just a month before, I had made one of the most important decisions of my life. On August 27, 2005, I decided to quit drinking. Although I had made several attempts before and had broken many promises to myself and others, that day I had reached the point of realizing that I simply could not be a social drinker any longer. There had been too many times when drinking to relax or have fun had turned into a hangover, regardless of how much water I drank or how much I tried to moderate it. I knew something had to change. So a month before embarking on a three-month sabbatical and two weeks in Italy, I quit drinking and began the long process of recovery, which in truth never ends. Recovery has now become part of my spiritual practice: a lifelong love affair with clarity, sobriety, and sanity. Now, my program is no longer about active recovery; it's about trying to practice the Twelve Steps in all my affairs and to be a presence for others who are struggling with addiction and recovery.

This book was born out of our desire to hear from fellow Unitarian Universalists about their recovery as it relates to the Twelve Steps of Alcoholics Anonymous. We acknowledge that the Twelve-Step program is not for everyone. Many Unitarian Universalists struggle with the overt God language of AA and its explicit assumption that one must have a Higher Power in order to fully recover. We also acknowledge that there are several other successful recovery programs that do not rely on a Higher Power, such as Rational Recovery, SMART Recovery, and LifeRing. However, our experiences have been with the Twelve Steps of Alcoholics Anonymous. This book represents the voices of women and men in active recovery, primarily from alcohol, drug, and food addictions. We could not represent the entire spectrum of addiction in this brief collection of essays; instead, we acknowledge that all addictions have similar issues and concerns: to stop the addictive pattern and begin a journey of recovery without being enslaved by addictive thinking and behavior.

We hope that the voices presented here will add to a conversation that's already taking place in Unitarian Universalist culture. The interconnections between Unitarian Universalism and the Twelve Steps have been occurring for decades in our church basements, at coffee hours, in small groups, from pulpits, through congregational addictions and recovery ministries, and, especially in the last ten years, on the pages of the *UU World* magazine and online. We respect the fact that for some Unitarian Universalists the Twelve-Step language of God and Higher Power just does not work. Yet many UUs have made and are making life-changing and spiritually enriching connections between these two traditions that place an emphasis on the formation of our character and our ethical behavior, and that attend to the reality of human pain and healing in the here and now.

The healing stories in this book are told from a first-person perspective but are not just about individual lives. Addiction is as much a reality for family and loved ones as it is for the addicts themselves. Ultimately, the fruits of the recovery journey are manifested in community—within families, in friendships, and in congregational life—and in our ability to grow strong bonds of health, peacefulness, and wholeness. We hope that this book will strengthen UU family and congregational life, and the larger interdependent web in and through which our lives take place.

In this same spirit of opening up conversation and breaking down barriers, we include a glossary at the back of this book that contains common Twelve-Step lingo. As with all cultures, the recovery movement uses its own language with which you may or may not be familiar. Please refer to the glossary as needed.

To all the sick and suffering alcoholics and addicts still out there, we dedicate this book and hope that the stories they find here may inspire them to seek recovery. And for those who have chosen the path of recovery, we hope that they will find support and courage for this lifelong journey.

In faith, hope, and love,

Ken and Cathlean

On Anonymity

The Twelve Steps are most often associated with anonymity. The founders of Alcoholics Anonymous originally conceived of the commitment to anonymity to assure maximum safety, trust, and unity among people in recovery, and to provide protection from a larger culture that often shamed or judged addicted people as inherently morally deficient. Anonymity remains a spiritual bedrock of the recovery journey. No one in recovery should feel compelled to reveal their identity against their wishes.

Currently, there are ongoing debates within the larger recovery community about the best way to honor the tradition of anonymity given the ubiquity of social media and an increasing emphasis on vulnerability, authenticity, and truth-telling in relationships. Some of the writers in this book believe strongly that complete anonymity about being in recovery adds to the stigmatization and marginalization of active or recovering addicts. Other contributors hold fast to the practice that anonymity should always be maintained in printed or public form.

We are not aiming to resolve that discussion here. For the sake of consistency, we are using first names only for all of our authors, following the common practice in recovery culture. Some of the writers in this book have decided to use their actual first names, and some have decided to use a pseudonym of their choice.

We respect both decisions. Learning to engage differences in life experience and perspective in an open and affirming way is an essential part of being Unitarian Universalist. As UUs, we know that there can be healthy diversity within a larger unity that holds and encourages us. This book reflects that commitment. These are all stories of lives transformed, whether they are offered with pseudonyms or actual names. The experience, strength, and hope contained in these stories speak for themselves.

Restored to Sanity

The Twelve Steps of Alcoholics Anonymous

1. We admitted we were powerless over alcohol—that our lives had become unmanageable.

2. Came to believe that a Power greater than ourselves could restore us to sanity.

3. Made a decision to turn our will and our lives over to the care of God *as we understood Him.*

4. Made a searching and fearless moral inventory of ourselves.

5. Admitted to God, to ourselves, and to another human being the exact nature of our wrongs.

6. Were entirely ready to have God remove all these defects of character.

7. Humbly asked Him to remove our shortcomings.

8. Made a list of all persons we had harmed, and became willing to make amends to them all.

9. Made direct amends to such people wherever possible, except when to do so would injure them or others.

10. Continued to take personal inventory and when we were wrong promptly admitted it.

11. Sought through prayer and meditation to improve our conscious contact with God *as we understood Him*, praying only for knowledge of His will for us and the power to carry that out.

12. Having had a spiritual awakening as the result of these steps, we tried to carry this message to alcoholics, and to practice these principles in all our affairs.

The Twelve Traditions of Alcoholics Anonymous

1. Our common welfare should come first; personal recovery depends upon AA unity.

2. For our group purpose there is but one ultimate authority—a loving God as He may express Himself in our group conscience. Our leaders are but trusted servants; they do not govern.

3. The only requirement for AA membership is a desire to stop drinking.

4. Each group should be autonomous except in matters affecting other groups or AA as a whole.

5. Each group has but one primary purpose—to carry its message to the alcoholic who still suffers.

6. An AA group ought never endorse, finance, or lend the AA name to any related facility or outside enterprise, lest problems of money, property, and prestige divert us from our primary purpose.

7. Every AA group ought to be fully self-supporting, declining outside contributions.

8. Alcoholics Anonymous should remain forever non-professional, but our service centers may employ special workers.

9. AA, as such, ought never be organized; but we may create service boards or committees directly responsible to those they serve.

10. Alcoholics Anonymous has no opinion on outside issues; hence the AA name ought never be drawn into public controversy.

11. Our public relations policy is based on attraction rather than promotion; we need always maintain personal anonymity at the level of press, radio, and films.

12. Anonymity is the spiritual foundation of all our traditions, ever reminding us to place principles before personalities.

Step One

We admitted we were powerless over alcohol—
that our lives had become unmanageable.

O Great Love,
For Defeat,
For Being Licked,
For Being Sick and Tired of Being Sick and Tired,
For Giving Up,
For Enough Finally Being Enough,
For the Path of Descent That Finally Reaches the Place
*   Known as the Bottom,*
I am profoundly grateful.

Unmanageable

John

My name is John, and I am a recovering alcoholic. This means that I have an incurable disease that I can manage but can never be rid of without further medical advances. But I can control my disease by not drinking alcohol. That seems simple now that I am sober, but it was bewildering when I was drinking. When I was under the addictive, cunning power of alcohol, I lied to myself in so many ways that the truth became impossible to recognize. My life became increasingly devoted to alcohol—dawn to dark—and well, yes, unmanageable.

Now, after some forty years of alcohol abuse since the age of eleven, and thankfully more than a decade of sobriety since then, I can manage to say it: I am powerless over alcohol, and I surrender. I had heard it countless times in AA meetings. Surrender implied that I could stop fighting alcohol and turn my addiction over to a Higher Power—God for some, the universe for others. But at its core was a primal cry for help that I was unwilling and, in retrospect, unable to make.

I fought, like so many struggling alcoholics do, to be able to keep on drinking. I fought to prove that I could have alcohol and limit my intake, that I could maintain a healthy body weight, blood pressure, and cholesterol level, and be spiritually connected to my family and my world. In short, I fought to show that I could have my alcohol and not be an alcoholic. Of course, I utterly lost the fight, and instead of turning to a Higher Power, I turned even more to alcohol. I was becoming more and more at risk, and I had no idea it was happening.

My first memory of alcohol comes from childhood. When I was three or four, my father gave me whiskey at bedtime for a cough. I can still taste it. By eleven, I was stealing drinks from my parents' liquor cabinet. By thirteen, I was grabbing cases of beer off Baltimore back porches with my friends, stashing them in the woods nearby for weekend parties. My drinking progressed unabated—teen years, college, graduate school, marriage, children —for years beer, then moving to gin, or in a pinch on a Sunday night, cooking wine and mouthwash. By my mid-thirties, it showed—a gut, puffy red face, disturbing medical reports. But the craving continued. By now it involved early morning drinking, multiple liquor stores, hiding the booze in my car, garage, basement. I told myself, my wife and children, and anyone else who asked that there was nothing to be concerned about. I was publishing scientific articles, getting grants. I was an avid runner and tennis player. "As long as I can do all that," I said earnestly, "how can alcohol be a problem?"

By my mid-forties, I was a raging, florid alcoholic. No one, not even I, knew or could even imagine how much I was actually drinking. My daily routine was to play tennis at 7:00 a.m. Then, with my wife off to work and the children at school, I'd return to an empty house and gulp as much wine as I could possibly consume before driving to work, then down some more wine in the car. I drank constantly in my office throughout the day and then came home to . . . what else? Steady drinking, of course. I was a mess.

After having lied to my doctor through many physicals, I finally confessed a bit of my dilemma to him—though nothing near the real truth. Like many general practitioners, mine knew little of the disease and was not particularly trained to recognize it. At first, he advised me to "cut back," "savor the wine," "drink slowly," "stop after two glasses." Fat chance. It took several more physicals with worsening numbers before his alarm caused him to act. He decisively took my arm and led me to the office of a substance abuse counselor. But that was only the beginning of my journey to sobriety. In fact, it took two more years of counseling and AA before I would surrender. During that time, my drinking got worse.

My counselor was great. If you are reading this as an active alcoholic, I can only hope that you will find someone like him. Against his better judgment, he worked with me for an entire year while I continued to drink and refused to go to AA. He was frustrated but stuck with me. Finally, because of his persistence, I consented to try AA. One of my fellow youth group adult advisors, a good friend, offered to drive me. He continued to go to meetings with me for an entire year.

It took the combination of my friend, my counselor, and AA to make it to recovery. I needed all that help because alone I was powerless against this relentless enemy. But my road to recovery was still a long one. I was drinking constantly, even on my way to AA meetings. Nonetheless, I slowly began to pay attention when the other members, one after another, told their stories. It began to dawn on me that no matter who was speaking at a meeting—a single mother from the New Haven projects, a postal worker, a university scientist—their stories were remarkably similar to mine. We were all powerless toward alcohol, and our lives had become unmanageable. And although we were a diverse group with widely different life experiences, we were collectively describing the same phenomenon: a disconnection from our loved ones and our world. The speakers had said this over and over in many different ways, but it took me a long time to grasp it.

Like all addictions, alcoholism is a disease of the spirit. Not only the times when I was drinking, but also the in-between times, were filled with cravings and devoted to strategies for getting the next drink. Alcohol had rendered me emotionally blunt, absent.

And then, without warning or forethought, it happened—I surrendered—and in an utterly surprising way. On a Thursday evening in late January, while getting ready to leave for choir rehearsal, I inexplicably threw my glass of wine out the door into the night. It had taken countless hours of counseling and AA meetings, but I haven't picked up another drink since. At this writing, it has now been twenty-four sober years of remarkable peace and gratitude.

If you attend AA, you will likely have heard the promises that are read at the beginning of meetings. It is promised that achieving sobriety will bring unexpected and amazing improvements to your life. Your life will become wonderfully manageable, and you will be rewarded in many surprising ways. You will experience broader feelings—deeper love, more joy, and yes, more sorrow too. You will begin to see and comprehend the world as never before, with wonderful, breathtaking clarity. Yes, the promises are real. They really come true.

I try to follow the Twelve Steps daily. But the first one is my personal mantra and never far from my thoughts. I am powerless over alcohol. I am so grateful to surrender to this profound truth.

Powerless

Gail

Powerless over alcohol? I'd never heard anything so stupid. Alcohol was power. Alcohol made all things possible. Alcohol made me physically strong, emotionally resilient, intellectually brilliant. Heck, without alcohol I'd be a mess. Powerless? Not exactly!

It started strong for me. I was never a social drinker. I came from a line of folks who drank daily, never got drunk, and never missed a day's work. I did all the cute kid things of sipping here and there when the adults were drinking. It was just curiosity at first.

When I was thirteen, all hell broke loose. The hormones hit. I realized very, very clearly that I was gay, and society wasn't. School became blazingly hard. And I responded with the same skills I'd seen working so well all around me. I started drinking alcohol. Procurement was easy. I stole it. And I bought it. No one carded tall middle-class white kids in the 1960s. I was off and running as an arrogant, know-it-all, rationalizing, daily drinker from the beginning.

I went past all the signposts of unmanageability so fast I could barely read the words. I chose the college I attended because of the state's eighteen-year-old drinking limit. Once I was there, while comrades sipped beers from shared pitchers, we always ordered a separate pitcher just for me. It seemed that the more I drank, the more serious and clearheaded I appeared. I behaved as though I were fearless. I did dumb and illegal things just to ward off boredom—or was it to prove I was alive or to pray I'd get caught? I was screaming for help, but not in a way that anyone could hear.

In one foray, I stole three gallon-bottles of cheap red wine from the local liquor store just to impress the ladies. One of my nicknames was "the Artful Dodger." God knows what other things I got called behind my back! Once, while my buddy was driving a Volkswagen van, I climbed out the passenger window and stood on the front bumper just to enjoy the breeze. While roommates sipped diet sodas to encourage term paper writing, I curled around a bottle of Jack Daniels to court the muse.

The well-thought-out preppy clothing I'd brought to college was quickly replaced by jeans and black turtlenecks. When former friends no longer wanted to hang out with increasingly crazy me, I rationalized that they were losers. They had no imagination, no sense of adventure. I stopped frequenting the clean and respectable campus pubs and moved further downtown to find the sawdust and sleaze of beer joints, where folks would think I was cool.

I left college without graduating. Graduation was for losers. I went into business for myself. God knows what work I was doing during the day to keep my parents and landlords distracted. It was all a smoke screen for my passion, my obsession, my addiction. I was dealing drugs. This well-educated, loved, and cared-for middle-class girl from the Boston suburbs was carrying a .45 caliber pistol and trading sanity for cocaine in New York City.

Cocaine makes everything move fast. One minute I'm dealing quarter-grams to college graduates, the next I'm a guest of the FBI for an overnight cruise through Riker's Island Women's Penitentiary in New York, arrested on suspicion of dealing narcotics and dangerous drugs. But off we were again the next day, free and clear. Saved by sexism! The district attorney was shocked that I and my four-foot-eleven butch lesbian business partner were not working with the large drug ring they were tracking in Miami. He gave us a lecture about watching the kind of company we kept and sent us back uptown.

Yikes! That was a close one. I sure learned a lot that night in prison. First, I learned that people coming down off heroin do amazing things when the drug starts to wear off. I learned that middle-class white girls have a very, very different experience in the holding cells than the brown-, black-, and tan-skinned girls from the city's rougher neighborhoods. We got pity and a few lectures on etiquette and advice about not wasting our futures. The other girls got propositioned, spit on, vilified, harassed, and otherwise treated like cockroaches. I'd have to wait for sobriety and wellness before I could begin to unpack that graduate-level seminar on real life.

Next I learned that cops and the feds got all excited when you had drugs on you or in you, so the lesson was clear: Stay away from drugs! I went from a seven-gram-a-day cocaine habit straight back to Mother Alcohol. Nobody messed with a functional drunk in those days. Alcohol welcomed me back with open arms.

It was time to settle down and start a family. I was out of work, so I went back to school and got a degree that would guarantee employability. I bought a car. Moved in with a girlfriend who had a house in the suburbs. Landed a series of respectable jobs and made the transition back from the underworld to the middle class. No one seemed to care if I drank at lunch as long as I did my job. No one seemed to notice that I did a half-assed job at work. After all, I was a master storyteller, a trained liar, and an experienced purveyor of excuses.

The lies I told to excuse poor performance, missed work, and slipped deadlines were just plausible enough to skim beneath most employers' radar. When things went wrong, it was never my fault. It was other people who screwed up, not me. Events beyond my control forced me into situations. My car had flat tires all the time. I was smart enough not to kill off grandparents too often. I helped myself along by switching jobs often enough to re-use my repertoire of excuses.

When I ran out of jobs, I went back to school. I became an alcohol snob. I stopped swilling rotgut cheap wine and started attending expensive wine-tasting events. I couldn't be a drunk—I only sipped top-shelf stuff. I was in seminary, on the vestry of a suburban-Boston Episcopal church, and drove a Volvo. No drunk, me. Also, never far from booze, me. I obsessed about alcohol. I planned my days around my drinking. I rode a motorcycle but never drank on two wheels, I was proud to boast. I also never let the engine cool off after a run before washing the bugs off my teeth with a cold one or two.

I had two decades of slamming my body and my spirit with drugs and alcohol before I had a jackpot I couldn't write off. A jackpot is an event most social drinkers don't have, it's a moment when you're supposed to be ashamed or frightened enough to reconsider your drinking and pull back. For me, jackpots were like notches in a gunfighter's pistol handle. Each time I rationalized, explained, excused, lied, slithered, and twisted my way out of bearing full responsibility for the chaos of my life, it reinforced how cool I was. I was a legend in my own mind!

Until I wasn't. I had been assisting the bishop at the altar of our church as we rededicated the building. My job was to carry the consecrated wine through the tiny sacristy, out the rear door, and pour it carefully beneath the trees in the side yard. Not rocket science, not hard to understand. It was something that had value for me. I didn't believe that the consecrated wine was supernatural or changed in any way. I just believed that it deserved deep respect. I had no doubt I was in control of my life. I was running the show. Until I wasn't.

I carried the wine into the sacristy, and before I could cross the small room, I'd upended the pitcher and poured it all down my throat. I was so horrified, I continued out the door, knelt next to the trees, and wept. I was sick at heart in a way I'd never fully felt through all the jackpots from drugs, through all the craziness and wild rides. I was morally bankrupt, and I had run out of excuses. I could clearly see what I was doing. I was bereft, disgusted, defeated.

But I wasn't done drinking. I knew, still, that my only hope was alcohol. I knew I could survive only if I could drink. The booze no longer worked to mask my despair. And I still drank. I went off into many more months of a blue haze, where the booze didn't work, but I kept on drinking. I was physically sick. I couldn't hold down the booze any longer. So I threw up, then drank more. Threw up, drank more.

Alcohol had me wired backward. The tighter my grip, the less I could hold on to what mattered. As I slithered down the progressive stages of addiction, I grew rigidly certain that my salvation required me to grab tighter, grip harder, and control more. Alcohol was my only hope. Until, of course, it wasn't.

My girlfriend's therapist got me admitted to a treatment center. It was Easter weekend. I was so brain-fogged and hallucinating that I actually "saw" words above the door to the clinic. The imaginary sign read, "Abandon Hope Ye Who Enter." Backward, I had it all backward. Hope came when I let go my grip on trying to control my life. Hope poured into my heart and my beleaguered mind when I let go of trying to manage situations and learned to tell the truth. Hope came when I was able just to admit out loud that my life had become unmanageable. I was powerless over alcohol.

Step Two

Came to believe that a Power greater than ourselves could restore us to sanity.

Gracious God—my Silent Companion,
I know I cannot do this alone.
I need the power that is greater than myself
to restore my life to sanity.

Spirit of Life, let the power of recovery and the community
work on my resistance to change.

A Power Greater Than Self

Andrea

Frustrated by continuing struggles in my significant relationships, on February 26, 2008, I attended my first Co-Dependents Anonymous meeting. I had previously had two years of therapy, talking about what I called my superiority complex and my amazing ability to understand where my character defects came from. During that time, the thought that my life was unmanageable never crossed my mind. In fact, my ability to control relationships with others and my perception that I was better than everyone around me gave me quite an ego boost.

The dynamic in my relationship with my partner of five years had started to bother me. I policed her spending, nagged her about her health, and criticized her lack of motivation to do almost everything that I knew would be helpful. The relationship felt one-sided. I was tired of feeling like a parent to her; however, my attempts to break that pattern through sheer willpower and couples therapy were unsuccessful. The dynamic was also bothering my partner, and it seemed unlikely that the relationship could last much longer. The time had come to find an approach other than therapy. When I was honest with myself, the dynamics of all my relationships were bothering me, and the common denominator was none other than me.

I had been attending meetings of Overeaters Anonymous (OA) in an attempt to gain some sanity around my annual diet and weight-loss adventures. It was in an OA meeting that I first heard about Co-Dependents Anonymous (CoDA). Back in high school, I called myself codependent to justify my constant jumping from relationship to relationship, so the word felt familiar to me.

Codependence manifests itself in many different ways. At CoDA meetings, we are offered a list of patterns and characteristics to help us identify our codependent behaviors. Unhealthy patterns of denial, compliance, low self-esteem, and control have been present throughout my life, impacting my ability to form healthy, loving relationships with others and with myself.

At that first meeting, I knew I was codependent. The topic of conversation focused on how feeling being better than or less than people around us were symptoms of a spiritual void. I left that meeting hoping that working the Twelve Steps could help me work through the issues that years of therapy and introspection hadn't.

The primary themes for me then tended to be—and still are—related to my controlling behaviors and low self-esteem. I devoted a lot of time and energy into being a leader in a local choir, both in my vocal section and on the board of directors. From the outside, I looked confident and successful, but often my actions and interactions were attempts to control how others perceived me. I could artificially feel better about myself when I was highly respected by my peers.

The fundamental flaw in this behavior was that I was rarely being my authentic self. Earning the respect of others meant maintaining a facade of perfection and an air of superiority. This kept me distant from most people in the choir. The relationships I formed tended to be superficial and based on my role as a leader in the organization. Being needed by the other singers made me feel important and significant.

My relationships with my closest friends were also difficult. Being around me often meant being around my moodiness when I wasn't getting my way. I often dominated conversations with stories of my greatness. If a friend would share a story about herself, I would add my personal anecdote to the conversation, never bothering to ask questions to get to know her better. This pattern was another manifestation of how I would attempt to control my relationships. I thought that I had *the* perfect advice to solve her problem, or that because I had done something better or survived something more challenging, she would be indebted to me. My sense of worth came from what I was doing and what my friends thought about those things. Without my activities and the apparent approval of my friends, I felt lonely and insecure. When I accepted these and other signs that my life was unmanageable, I admitted my powerlessness in Step One and moved on to Step Two.

The most important word in Step Two is not *believe*, as one might expect; rather, it is *came*. Coming to believe is a process—a journey rather than a destination. For me, this journey involves many little choices and decisions that are often difficult to make. At each critical moment though, I find the courage to just trust—trust in the adventure, in the universe, in the instinct that is pushing me out of my comfort zone and into the unknown.

Shortly after I started attending CoDA meetings, I recognized that I had more opportunities than I could have imagined to practice new behaviors. In this process, I truly came to believe that a power greater than myself could restore me to sanity.

My involvement in the choir came to an abrupt halt. I had a conflict that interfered with the annual December concert and so I opted to stop attending rehearsals in September. I didn't know who I was outside of that organization, and my interactions with my fellow singers were often my only social outlet. To make the change, I had to trust that I would rediscover myself after giving up this key contributor to my sense of worth. Letting this commitment go opened me up to new opportunities for growth and community that would not previously have been possible. Although I was scared to give up that activity, I now find it difficult to imagine going back.

With my friends, the biggest changes have been my ability to go with the flow and to listen rather than talk. The hardest part about not constantly dominating the conversation is not knowing how to engage in a two-way conversation. Although for some people this skill comes easily, for me it is a struggle. I have to quiet my mind enough to pay attention and then also respond appropriately. My ability to practice this is definitely a gift from my Higher Power; left solely to my own devices, I would likely speak too much or remove myself entirely from the conversation.

Although I am still filled with anxiety in social situations, I do what I can to work through it. I am often up front with new friends about my anxiety; although talking about it doesn't make the anxiety go away, it removes some of the shame and embarrassment and keeps me humble. Too often in the past, my relationships were based on a false sense of superiority. Now being honest with people in my life provides opportunities to live authentically and without the mask I used to wear. My sense of worth is now derived more from the inside than the outside. I know that I can be myself regardless of what others think of me. I do not depend on their respect or admiration to feel good about myself.

When I have the instinct to practice new behaviors, I attribute this feeling to my Higher Power. As a Unitarian Universalist, I don't need a pinned-down concept of God in order to experience God. My UU identity allows me to look for the divine all around me. From something as small and real as a butterfly to something as abstract as a feeling of unconditional love, there is something miraculous, indeed divine, in every day and every situation I encounter.

I have been blessed to find a new UU congregation that challenges me to grow. It provides me with opportunities to continue my CoDA spiritual journey in the loving embrace of a supportive community. The connections that I find with other congregants are authentic and are additional manifestations of the divine in my life. I am often struck by a sense of awe and of being part of something larger than myself. The gift of this program is that, even as I recognize that I am just a single drop in an infinitely wide and deep well, I am also filled with a sense of spiritual fullness unlike any I've ever known.

It is from this place of fullness that I am eager to continue the journey of coming to believe. One day at a time, I find the willingness to trust that a power greater than myself can restore me to sanity.

Restored to Sanity

Paul

I started drinking in high school as a way to fit in. I was not a popular kid, but I wasn't one of those kids that got picked on either. Mostly, people simply didn't notice me. I was raised and grew up as a girl because that was my presenting physical reality, but my internal reality was very different. I was awkward, and although I didn't know it at the time, I was struggling to understand my gender and sexual orientation. Like many of my peers and friends, I liked boys, but I wanted to be one, not to kiss them. Growing up in rural New England, I didn't know what it meant to be a lesbian, and gender expression was not even close to my radar screen, much less on it. Maybe I was sheltered, or maybe I just didn't want to know. What I did know was that I didn't always fit in, that I felt somehow blurry compared to my friends. They all seemed to be finding themselves and each other in relationships while I continued to struggle. Drinking and using drugs allowed me to fit in. I figured out that to make friends or to be noticed by others, I only had to carry pot or alcohol and be willing to share.

Believing in a power greater than myself wasn't all that hard. I had grown up in a church where God and Jesus were both good guys for the most part, but my family had left the church in the early 1970s. It was a difficult time for me: My older brother was trying to discover his own sexual identity, and I was his laboratory. The sexual abuse started about the same time we stopped attending church, and at the age of eight, I connected those two events. I was sure we had stopped attending because of it and felt a great deal of shame—shame that I converted into anger and sarcasm toward the world around me. In college I came out as a lesbian, and I had enough dealings with churches to know that they did not support gay and lesbian people.

I developed a cynical, sarcastic view of life as a result of the sexual abuse and from living in a world in which I was not able to be myself. I was sure there was no reason to stick around in this world, because it had proven itself rather ugly. As a lesbian, I was sure that anything religious was just evil and that God, or any organized understanding of God, had to be corrupt and hypocritical. I felt that if God and Jesus really were the good guys of my childhood, I would not have been abandoned by them when we left the church.

When I first began attending recovery meetings, I understood that I had to let go of my cynicism. This was a crucial step, one that would provide the groundwork for the rest of my recovery. So I spent some time thinking about it. At first, I simply believed in the power of the group. The group helped me to focus on my recovery and to avoid "people, places, and things," i.e., triggers for addictive behaviors. The group also helped me to keep things simple and slow, because at that point, my life was a mess. I had destroyed most of my relationships, had damaged my academic career (the college had kicked me out for a GPA of 1.083), was in danger of losing my housing, and hated myself. Although I was passively suicidal, I was not actively so, and knew that I needed to make some changes or I really was going to kill myself. The insanity of my life included a never-ending cycle of guilt, shame, self-inflicted pain, and regret. I recall waking up one morning, not entirely sure where I was, or who I was with. I slowly realized that someone had urinated in the middle of the night, making a mess of the bed. I suspected it was me but figured that my behavior could be justified because I had been so drunk. I got up, walked into the bathroom, washed my face, cleaned up, and got dressed. I spent a minute or two trying to recall the name of the woman I had slept with and gave up. I decided the best course of action was to walk out of the bathroom and say good-bye. I left the house not entirely sure how I had gotten there, where my car was, or how I would get home. I walked outside and looked up and down the street, spotted my car, found my keys in my pocket, and left. That night I was out again, drinking and getting high, repeating the same pattern.

I woke each morning, went through my list of "I will nevers," and realized how many I had broken: I will never drink or use before noon, I will never drink or use alone, I will never go to class high, I will never steal, I will never. . . . This list had grown shorter and shorter over time. Each time, I had a perfectly reasonable justification for breaking one of my own rules.

The insanity of this cycle was deadly. Each time I broke a rule, I was filled with shame and drank or used to avoid the truth of life. Far from being fun, my life had become a blur, a desperate need to escape and to avoid feelings. I articulated my dreams of being a catalyst for change in a drunken stupor or drug-induced daze. At some point, I forgot them completely. The only thing that mattered was how I was going to afford or manipulate my way into getting my next drink or drug. I was good at getting my friends to buy me drinks, but I was often the one who supplied the drugs. I cashed checks on closed accounts, forged checks, and even embezzled money from a job I had. This cycle of more broken rules only fueled the need to stay unconscious. The insanity consumed my life.

The last straw was when I missed my girlfriend's dance performance, and none of my friends would speak to me. Something had to change. When I finally got to Twelve-Step meetings, I knew I had to make some changes. At first, the group did serve as my Higher Power, and over time my mind cleared a bit. I began to reconnect with something deeper and more meaningful inside myself. I had heard others talk about their anger at God, of their not wanting to be "pushed into believing," or converted to some cult. I felt the same way, but I knew if I was going to become sane, and move out of my shame and pain, I needed to recognize that I could not trust my own thought process and had to rely on someone or something else to guide me. The group's "good orderly direction" helped me to stay focused. As I listened to others, I heard my own shame and pain being articulated and began to understand that I was not alone, that I was not unique, that I could indeed get better. Something inside me began to stir, and I was reminded of my dreams of being a catalyst for change. I began to think that it was actually possible.

I talked in meetings, a lot, probably too much. I shared my struggles, spent time with my sponsor, and avoided old friends and habits. I took other peoples' advice and tried to stay out of my head. I looked for a Higher Power that I could accept. I began to explore world religions to try to find a more compelling Higher Power. The group, although helpful, did not meet my deeper spiritual needs. As I studied, I found that many evil things had been done in the name of religion, but I also discovered that religion could offer some good. Its lessons spoke to me. I began to discover some simple truths common in all religions and that many of these truths were values that I held—values from my childhood rekindled in recovery, values that I thought were being denied or ignored by organized religion. I found in my recovery that, rather than becoming discouraged and cynical because of my discoveries, I felt motivated to learn more. I believed at the time, and still do, that much of my sense of insanity was caused by feeling disconnected from God. The God I had been raised to believe in was a loving, caring, helpful God; a God who supported justice and mercy; a God who loved all creation; a God who did not judge people because of who they loved. The more I studied, the more I came to believe that such a God did exist. I began to trust again. I began to trust myself again. I began to feel sane again.

The God of my understanding has changed over the past twenty years of my sobriety. As I have changed and grown, my understanding of God has grown with me. I have explored Native traditions, Eastern philosophy, and even Christianity. The fundamental values and principles on which my God is grounded have not changed. I believe in the healing power of love. I believe that nature offers us a window into the sacred. I believe that grace happens. I believe that no matter what we've done, no matter how horrible or evil our action may have been (and I mean this truly, including rapists and murderers), we are still part of creation, and we still have worth and dignity. I believe that unconditional love and compassion are the ultimate goals of humanity, and I believe that we are all capable of achieving them. Peace has come to me through a regular practice of meditation and chanting. Daily inventories continue to guide me and shape the choices that I make. God, for me, is in the process of living and is a verb rather than a noun.

It has been over twenty years since I made choices based on how I could find my next drink or drug. I no longer wake up wondering how I got home, who I am with, or who it was that wet the bed. My sanity was restored by my willingness to be honest with myself, with others, and with a process of accepting the power of love and forgiveness in my life. Gratitude helps me stay sane each day.

Step Three

Made a decision to turn our will and our lives over to the care of God *as we understood Him*.

Dear God, I may not know You well, or at all, or even have the voice to speak Your name aloud.

But, somehow, I trust You.

Trust that I am held by You, who are greater than myself and loving enough to hold the harms I've caused and the hurt I've suffered.

Trust that I can turn to You for help.

Trust that in the very act of turning to Your larger presence that something shifts within me that invites new life to come forward.

Trust that trusting You is a step toward making myself trustworthy.

Trust that as I make space for You, I may find my voice and my place in this life.

Amen.

Made a Decision

Kent

As a lifelong Unitarian Universalist, this Step almost made me walk away from Alcoholics Anonymous. And yet, it eventually helped me tremendously to unlock the doors that were keeping me a prisoner within myself.

I entered the rooms of AA willing to try almost anything to reduce my pain, battling the chains of depression and alcoholism. People told me that this Step—turning our will and life over to the care of God as we understand him—is a great pain management tool. Although it was offered with the very best of intentions, I cringed when I first heard this approach. For me, the "Let go and let God" attitude evoked that of Catholic bishops in Latin America who worked on the side of the landed elite when they told the peasants, "Don't worry about your brutal poverty. This is God's plan. Let go and trust God, and you will receive your reward in heaven in the afterlife." It seemed to violate the teachings of Dr. Martin Luther King Jr. and so many other liberating spiritual teachers, who encouraged us to challenge injustice and change our world for the better.

Religion, philosophy, and recovery all raise important questions about power. In this precious, crazy, beautiful, worrisome world, who has the power? Who or what makes things happen, and how? Because of life's pervasive lack of fairness, I have always felt an aversion to theologies that claim that God is in charge of everything. I have heard it said more than once in the rooms of AA that "God controls all. We can't understand why some things happen. God has a larger plan in which we should trust." Viewing the world's suffering, I could never agree. God didn't cause all these problems. Human beings deserved much of the blame. Similar objections cause many Unitarian Universalists to struggle with the Third Step.

During the first couple of months after I found AA, I investigated other options, programs without this kind of God language. Over time, I have realized that Alcoholics Anonymous is the best game in town. This holds true for many agnostics, atheists, and persons of progressive spirituality. Once I realized that I didn't have to agree theologically with AA literature or all the folks in the rooms in order to get better and grow, I began to feel at home with AA. I learned to put aside the metaphysical and ontological debates about God. I took comfort in knowing that every time the literature refers to God it always stipulates that it is God as each individual person understands God.

In many places, AA literature refers to God as a man: Him. This has never resonated with me or made any sense. I translate this language in a way that respects my spiritual integrity.

Early in my recovery, I had a good AA friend who was comfortable enough with himself that he often wore his biking shorts and helmet in the meetings. Gene was impressively dedicated to service. He taught me about a core element of the Third Step when he said—often—that the only thing you have to know about God is that you are not God. I felt like I was buried in an avalanche of pain, and I didn't know if any rescue teams would be able to find me. I knew I wasn't God.

The Third Step encouraged me to reflect on my beliefs and on that to which I dedicated myself. I came to believe that God is love and love is God. I believe that there are divine energies of love, courage, and hope in this world that are infinitely greater than I.

As a Unitarian Universalist, I draw upon a rich tapestry of theology that helps us to understand our human relationship with divine mystery and to engage in collaborative efforts to fortify justice. We never have to settle for the concept of a separate God who operates over and above us. Ralph Waldo Emerson said that all human beings are connected to God through a transcendent OverSoul. The eighteenth- and nineteenth-century Universalist evangelist Judith Sargent Murray proclaimed the oneness of divinity with the "spirits of the human race." Twentieth-century Unitarian theologian Henry Nelson Weiman said that God was creativity itself. Universalists and Unitarians have boldly proclaimed that divine powers are within all of creation, including humans. God blesses bountifully and loves every person. Ultimately, I don't know if these statements are metaphors, mysteries, or just well-intentioned guesses about life. Many people wish to call the divine by the names *community*, *light*, *nature*, *joy*, or *spirit of life*. They all work for me.

This leads to the next aspect of the Third Step. What does it mean to turn our lives over to the care of God—or light, love, joy, or nature? Nature itself is indifferent to human beings. Bad things happen to good people all the time. Many of us have wondered why we should risk "turning ourselves over" to a chaotic, unfair universe.

I have come to believe that there is a gracious goodness in AA groups, the church, the community, and the world. If we open ourselves up (or plug ourselves in), we can benefit greatly. When I pray, count my blessings, celebrate life, and help others, I gain strength. On the other hand, when I seek revenge, lament my losses, only look inward, and sulk, I become weaker. Counterintuitively, when I open my heart and turn myself over to the world, I am stronger than if I just rely on self-sufficiency.

I know that my experience is similar to many recovering alcoholics in the program. Over time, I have come to new understandings and appreciations of the power of letting go. Some of the periods in my life when I have experienced the most profound happiness have come directly from the serenity of accepting things

I cannot change. I have gone days, and in some cases weeks, when the answer to any dilemma I experienced was to let go. Whether it is a small thing or a big thing, I have just said to myself, "Stop thinking about it and trying to control it." Then I become less weighed down and more able to live and appreciate life.

The Third Step reminds me of the beauty and power that I find in the Serenity Prayer: "God, grant me the serenity to accept the things I cannot change, the courage to change the things I can, and the wisdom to know the difference." The Third Step encourages us to let go of those things that no longer serve us. Letting go of what we cannot or should not try to control brings forth the best in us, facilitates connections with others, and increases our appreciation for the miracles and majesty of life. Alcoholics Anonymous and Unitarian Universalism both point us to "a faith that works." I try to work the Third Step every day by doing what I can and letting go of that which is not mine to hold.

Turning Over Our Will

Julie

A spiritual path was the last thing I expected to find when I entered the rooms of Alcoholics Anonymous to learn how to stop drinking in 2003. After all, I was fifty-three years old, the mother of two daughters, the wife of a fire captain in a large metropolitan fire department, an appellate lawyer, and an equestrian. My outlook on life was pretty well set by then. I hadn't attended church since I was seventeen, when the youth minister in the Presbyterian church our family halfheartedly attended harshly rebuffed my curious inquiries with (what sounded to me like), "There's only one god—and we have him." I went on to college in the late 1960s, reveled in the freedom from the "ignorance" of my elders, was introduced to alcohol in a big way, and wholeheartedly rejected anything to do with God or religion.

About thirty-five years later, I learned that God was not owned by the church of my youth, and spirituality was something different from religion. I was introduced to these liberating notions because I went to AA and worked the Twelve Steps, and because, in doing that work, I discovered and became involved with Unitarian Universalism. I went to AA to learn how to stop drinking. However, what AA taught me, via the Steps, was how to live my life on life's terms. And in that process, I had to grapple with the concepts of God, spirituality, my place on the planet, and my reason for being, to name a few. For help working through these concepts, I turned to Unitarian Universalism. The Twelve Steps and the Unitarian Universalist Principles combined to provide me a design for living that works.

For those thirty-five years in between, I was what many people —including myself and the family I grew up in—refer to as a "social drinker" who now and then drank too much. I would go for stretches without drinking at all (thereby proving to myself I didn't have a problem), and it didn't occur to me to drink when I was pregnant. However, on the inside, I was different. From my first half glass of beer in college, I'd always wanted to keep drinking once I started. In fact, I thought everyone did and had to exercise great restraint and willpower to say that they'd had enough. What I didn't realize was that I was genetically wired to be an alcoholic and that, like many people, I used alcohol to manage stress, pain, unhappiness—anything that caused unpleasant feelings I didn't want to acknowledge or didn't know how to handle.

When I finally realized I needed help, the outward trappings of my life remained intact, but I had emotionally hit bottom. My older sister had died of lung cancer eight months earlier, after a short illness. Drinking no longer worked as a means of avoiding emotional pain. Once I opened that first beer when I got home from work, I couldn't stop drinking until I went to bed. No matter what my intentions were at the beginning of each day, I popped open that beer every night—and I could never, ever have just one.

So I (feebly) took action. I went to a few AA meetings, cannily thinking I could avoid the whole God thing and just learn how to stop drinking; I entered an outpatient chemical dependency treatment center. But, ho-ho, big surprise, we had to work the Twelve Steps! *And* go to AA! And that's what saved my life. The First Step was no problem for me. It seemed quite clear that I was powerless over alcohol and my life was unmanageable—I was there at the treatment center, right? That seemed like a pretty good clue to me. The Second Step was more difficult, but because it used the words *Power greater than ourselves*, and not *God*, I could get through it. The big stumbling block was Step Three.

Step Three says, "Made a decision to turn our will and our lives over to the care of God *as we understood Him.*" My reaction: You want me to decide to turn *what* over to *whom*? The Step contains italicized words—very important in understanding what the writers of the Big Book emphasized. In all the steps, the only italicized phrase—in Steps Three and Eleven—is "*as we understood Him.*" The writers were emphasizing our freedom to determine how we understood God. But, like many of us who focus on what we don't believe as opposed to what we do believe or what we could possibly believe, I only latched onto the word *Him*. And my mind, all on its own, italicized *our will*, *our lives*, and *God*, convincing me that this Step was screaming that I must become a helpless blob and mindlessly follow some male god's orders. Of course, I balked. This was clearly unacceptable.

But I did not want to go back to that stark, powerless place where I'd been—and the Steps seemed to be working for those women I knew and admired in AA. So I kept plugging along. One of the Big Book meetings I attended was a real "God" meeting: God this, God that. And when it was my turn to lead, I *always* got the spirituality topics. I was constantly frustrated, complaining, "I don't get it," when it came to the Higher Power and Third Step concepts, suggesting that perhaps these spirituality topics would be better assigned to someone who *did* get it. But even the women in this rather God-focused meeting didn't push me to believe a certain way. They told me I just had to be honest, open, and willing concerning the spirituality issue. I listened to them and to my sponsor and heavily relied on Herbert Spencer's quote in Appendix II of the Big Book, "Spiritual Experience": "There is a principle which is a bar against all information, which is proof against all arguments and which cannot fail to keep a [person] in everlasting ignorance—that principle is contempt prior to investigation." I'd always prided myself on being open-minded, so I figured I'd better be what I thought I was. I started investigating.

And this is where Unitarian Universalism came into the picture. I remembered that, a few years earlier, a colleague of mine had told me about a church that I might find interesting. She'd discovered it when she and her husband were looking for a church after their daughter was born. She assured me that it did not espouse any dogma and was very welcoming. I called her and asked about it again—it was a Unitarian Universalist church just a few miles from my house. I started attending and discovered a warm, supportive group of people who were socially aware and active, and open to new ideas. Generally, they seemed to tend toward atheism, agnosticism, and intellectualism, but they also were open to the exploration of spirituality.

I had always thought the only way to have a spiritual life was to connect to a recognized and established religion. I learned in AA that this was not true. Many people in AA have full and complete spiritual lives via the Twelve Steps and the AA program alone. But I felt I needed help with these spiritual concepts that I had never contemplated in any depth, particularly since discovering the intellectual world of the law. At a Twelve-Step seminar, I heard a kind, impish, and lovable priest with umpteen years of sobriety say that a religion is simply the "furniture" of a spiritual life, a way of expressing a spiritual experience. It is the means by which someone can share their spiritual experience, to create an opening for love.

When I looked at the seven Principles, I thought that Unitarian Universalism might be the perfect "furniture" for my spiritual life. I believed first and foremost in the inherent worth and dignity of every human being, and that first Principle drew me to the church. In AA, we learn, often for the first time, that *we alcoholics* have inherent worth and dignity. Once we understand this about ourselves at the deepest level, we *know* the first Principle. It's in our bones. For me, it's also a feeling of interconnection. "Thou art that," as mythologist Joseph Campbell says. We're capable of compassion and can feel for each other because we *are* each other, which is for me the seventh Principle. And we understand the first and seventh Principles on this level through the free and responsible search for truth and meaning described by the fourth Principle. The open search is not just allowed in Unitarian Universalism but actually promoted as a vital Principle. What a concept! Quite different from my experience in the church I attended as a teenager. The first, fourth, and seventh Principles helped me realize I had found a spiritual home, and so I joined a Unitarian Universalist church.

In the fall of 2005, after the arrival of our new minister, the church launched an Addictions and Recovery Ministry (ARM), based upon Denis Meacham's model in his *Addictions Ministry Handbook*. By that time, I had completed the Twelve Steps with my AA sponsor, but I was still struggling with Step Three and unsatisfied with what I had come up with so far.

While on vacation in Carmel, California, my husband and I found an intriguing little bookstore, where I found some great books for ARM. The most notable was *The Five Things We Cannot Change . . . and the Happiness We Find by Embracing Them*, by David Richo. I began reading it, and as we drove home, it dawned on me that this book was my Third Step. Richo quoted Reinhold Niebuhr's prayer, commonly known as the Serenity Prayer, noting that it had become the cornerstone of the recovery movement: "God grant me the serenity to accept the things I cannot change, the courage to change the things I can, and the wisdom to know the difference." Richo identified the things we cannot change, i.e., the givens:

- Everything changes and ends.

- Things do not always go according to plan.

- Life is not always fair.

- Pain is part of life.

- People are not loving and loyal all the time.

If we live in denial of these givens, we live in pain and frustration. But if we can give an unconditional yes to them, we courageously align ourselves to reality. Richo writes, "Once we trust reality more than our hopes and expectations, our yes becomes an 'open sesame' to spiritual surprises."

The Five Things was my Third Step because I understood that turning my "will and my life over to the care of God" means accepting the givens of life and aligning myself with reality to be open to what life has to offer. I was with my sister Dianne when she died. I was forced to let her go when I wanted so much to hold on to her. I was absolutely and utterly without control. I had to accept her death and align myself with reality. Where the oft-spoken "God's will" makes absolutely no sense to me, and is even trite and dismissive, the wisdom from *The Five Things* began to make eminent sense, in my head and in my heart. So in a very fundamental way, and for the first time, I came to accept my sister's death. I understood.

The same colleague who told me about the Unitarian Universalist church has affected my spiritual journey more than once and provided me with one of those "spiritual surprises" that Richo talks about. She and I met for lunch to catch up and go to a gallery she'd been wanting to show me. As we wandered among the stones, statues, and books, listening to hauntingly beautiful chants, I picked up a little gift book called *Ganesh: Removing the Obstacles*. It was not a sacred text, just a small book explaining folk narratives and other material about Ganesh, the elephant-headed God of New Beginnings (among other titles) found in several Eastern religions. Even after my breakthrough with *The Five Things*, I was still struggling with what my Higher Power looked like. I so much wanted to have a personal god but had never experienced such a relationship. I thought I had arrived at what I believed, but it was so amorphous. An important insight came to me from that little gift book: I don't "turn my life and my will over" to an entity so much as "step into the flow of life." I feel connected to all of life when I live in the balance I find through the spiritual surprises made available to me when I try to live in accordance with the Twelve Steps—particularly the Third, the one I found the most difficult, even treacherous, to my way of thinking.

And that has been my startling discovery: Only through the individual spiritual journey can we find the real source of sobriety, our authentic selves. And now, because of my searching, I understand how to live while I am here—and how to live fully and completely, as best I can, without something like alcohol to shield me from life's realities. I can face them, walk through the harsh ones, relish the good ones, learn from the distressing ones, and not become hardened by them. This does not mean I don't try to avoid the harsh realities by other means (intellectualism, playing solitaire on the computer, or acting silly to be distracted come to mind) or don't find them painful or distressing. It just means I have a spiritual means and a circle of support with which to deal with them, for better or worse. I have learned to do the best job I can and leave the results to the universe.

While there are many things I can't control, there is something I can control. It's fairly simple. I can control my reactions, my responses to life. I can control the actions I take in living my life according to the concepts I've learned, and continue to learn, in and through Alcoholics Anonymous, Unitarian Universalism, and the rest of the world. As for the wisdom to know the difference, that just takes time, reflection, and very dear, wise friends and mentors. Most importantly, I know I don't have to solve any major problem on my own.

Step Four

Made a searching and fearless
moral inventory of ourselves.

*"Create in me a clean heart and renew a right spirit
within me," begins the Psalmist.*

*In moments of reflection and meditation, I examine the
thoughts, words, and deeds of my life.*

*I look at the harm that I have done to others in thought,
word, or deed.*

*I write them down in great detail, seeing and feeling the
consequences of my addiction.*

*I keep digging down, deeper, until my inventory is
complete.*

Rest with this list and with this Step.

In the silence of this moment, rest.

Searching and Fearless

Alex

My name is Alex and I am an alcoholic. That's how I introduce myself at Alcoholics Anonymous meetings, but usually that's not all I say. It's an important start, but that's not all I am, nor should my identity stop there.

Simple labels don't tell the whole story. When I was asked to write about Step Four, "Made a searching and fearless moral inventory of ourselves," I thought to myself, "This will be easy to do." I'm pretty good with words, and I have worked the Steps throughout the years since I became sober for the second time on June 14, 2003.

On June 13, I'd had my last drunk and blackout event. I'd hidden my drinking from the good people of the church where I'd completed a successful two-year interim ministry. I was ready to move back to the West Coast and continue my ministry and life. I would put all the mistakes and errors of my life in Illinois behind me.

Who was I really kidding, other than myself? Near that final day of active alcoholism, I'd opened my front door and seen the board president of the church sitting on my steps, waiting for me. He had come to my apartment out of worry that neither he nor my partner Debra in Oregon could reach me by phone. I remember his compassion but felt his disappointment. That memory stays with me now: I hit the wall of bottoming out and knowing I was powerless over my alcoholism. I'd had to withdraw myself from a successful candidacy at a church because of my relapses a month earlier. Who was I kidding?

I called my beloved, patient life partner, Debra, to tell her I'd had enough denial and lying to myself and others. I went to the AA meeting that I'd attended for months, but this time I was physically and emotionally sober.

Step Two had been there all along, and I knew there was a power greater than myself, although calling it God in the traditional sense made no sense to me. So the power greater than my small ego became that meeting on June 14 and the three folks from the church who helped me pack my belongings in a rental truck. That power became Debra, who was willing to let me stay at her home as we'd planned while I tried to sort out my life. The power greater than myself became a world of sober colors, sounds, voices, feelings, and vows.

Step Four really began as I started my long solitary journey west to Oregon. A full U-Haul truck towing a car on a trailer served as my home for four days. Friends from the AA community called me several times each day to make sure I was okay. An old friend in recovery was at a Zen retreat but broke the rule of silence each day to call me to see if I'd been to a meeting. They were welcome reminders of powers greater than myself as I drove past endless miles of corn and wheat fields and then sagebrush prairies. I had plenty of time to think about a searching and fearless moral inventory. It wasn't a new effort on my part. Each night at a motel, I'd write down whatever I could remember, starting with my childhood and moving through adolescence into adulthood.

By the time I reached Oregon and Debra's home, I'd been able to thrash my way through my childhood and early teen years. It was just the surface of a true inventory, but compared to my earlier efforts, it was more honest and soul-searching. All the while, I kept reminding myself to use the inventory as a moving, living spiritual practice.

At the beginning of this essay, I mentioned that I add more words to my introduction at AA meetings. These are the words I prefer to use: ". . . and I am an inherently whole person." I admit that adding these words sometimes gets me dirty looks or shaking heads. It's not the traditional introduction, so some feel it's an example of my resistance to the program. Yet, I cannot accept the traditional Judeo-Christian, 1930s gender-specific language of the Twelve Steps, and I would be dishonest if I didn't add that statement to the end of my introduction. Honesty, after all, is an essential part of living the Twelve Steps.

I am an alcoholic in recovery, and I am also a longtime practicing Buddhist. Buddhism teaches that we are inherently whole and complete, and that each of us has at our core the capacity to fully awaken to our true nature. This means that making a fearless and searching moral inventory ought to include not only the suffering we've caused others but also how we experience it ourselves. My sponsors in AA, along with my spiritual teachers in the Buddhist community, have agreed that making a fearless and searching moral inventory should become a spiritual practice like meditation or any mindfulness training.

After I arrived at Debra's, we worked hard to live together. I found a wonderful meeting that I still consider my home group. Several men offered to be my sponsor, but I chose to continue with a Buddhist friend who shared many of my beliefs about revised versions of the Steps.

I wrote and thought and wrote some more. In past years before relapsing, I'd written out a Fourth Step. I'd made amends to old girlfriends, my parents, and foster parents, friends whom I'd harmed in word or deed. Now I needed to look through that old inventory again and see what might be missing.

One of the great things about the Fourth Step is that the process helps us remember more and more about our past and fill in those blank spaces. This time, I remembered an event from childhood when I threw an ice cube at another child who wanted my toys. He's probably forgotten about it fifty years later; I have not. It's got to be on the list. I cannot make amends—make up for my behavior or offer an apology—to him, but I can remember how old anger can continue down the years. How much pain and fury I must have felt in the moment I threw that ice cube, and how wonderful that I remember my pain fifty years later. That memory tells me that I am a whole human being with all the flaws and blessings we carry.

I've mentioned one label—practicing Buddhist—in my list of aspirations and identities that make up Alex. Here's another one: someone who aspires to live honestly. The Fourth Step calls us to make a "searching and fearless moral inventory of ourselves." That means we need to look at our failings and mistakes first and own up to their effects on others. Then we need to see how such failings caused suffering for ourselves.

That takes a lot of truthfulness. A friend and admired Buddhist teacher, Kevin Griffin, writes in his book *One Breath at a Time* that the Fourth Step is about no-nonsense honesty. It is a practice in which we make rigorous and compassionate honesty the core of our sobriety, whether we are working the Steps or following some other spiritual discipline.

This brings me to a final label that I might add to my introduction at an AA meeting—I am also a Unitarian Universalist. That means that I try to live out the seven Principles and a theology based on inherent goodness rather than a broken, sinful humanity.

All too often, I hear people in meetings speak of their Fourth Step as a searching and fearless inventory of all their misdeeds, errors, and generally bad behaviors. As a Buddhist and Unitarian Universalist, I see that as only half the task of the Fourth Step. The other half is to create an inventory of our gifts, compassion, and good behaviors. A searching and fearless moral inventory cannot end only with immoral actions, words, or deeds from our lives. However honest that work is, it is only part of the story, and it is the dangerous part that could lead us back to our addiction. Adding a positive inventory can help us renew our faith in the First

Principle—inherent worth and dignity. It can remove the temptation to conclude that we are beyond redemption or renewal. That feeling of despair can easily lead us to relapse. It has happened to me and others I know in AA many times.

So my Fourth-Step inventory includes an inventory of all the positive words, thoughts, and deeds I can remember through the years. I do this part of my inventory last. It provides a gentle balance with all my mistakes so I can discover the full, rich nature of my relationships with others.

To help maintain my sobriety, my balanced Fourth-Step inventory continues to this day. I strive to be honest and trustworthy and to live my faith of inherent wholeness. The inventory has become a treasure trove of all the teachings in my life. Buddhist teacher Jack Kornfield has said, "Every person we meet is our greatest teacher, and everything that happens is a teaching."

Each item in the inventory reminds me of teaching I have received from someone about how important it is to recover and to heal. Each one is precious beyond measure and a gift I treasure. The Fourth Step has taken me from fear to fearlessness and from being lost to finding myself at last.

A Moral Inventory

Page

I feel an incredible sense of gratitude toward Bill W. and the many, many men and women who follow in his tradition of recovery from alcohol addiction. They helped my brother save his own life. Through daily AA meetings, the Steps, a sponsor, and an acceptance of a Higher Power, my brother is living a life of joyful recovery. The thrill of having him present again in my life is a gift I cherish on a daily basis—one for which I will be ever grateful.

One of the most striking parts of his sobriety is the impact it has had on me, in particular on my own spiritual development. He was going to get sober—about that I had no doubt. He was invested and committed, knowingly facing his own demons. I, on the other hand, was woefully unprepared for my journey as the sibling of someone in AA. I did not recognize the gaping holes in my own sense of self in the face of my loved one's recovery process.

I was first caught off guard when my agnostic brother readily accepted God as his keeper in his Fourth Step, in which he took a fearless moral inventory. His acceptance of a Higher Power was off-putting to my rational, academic way of thinking—a realm where I comfortably and successfully hid.

I grew up as an Episcopalian on the Main Line of suburban Philadelphia—the equivalent of the Bible Belt for WASPs. We didn't go to church except to attend big events like weddings and memorial services, and occasionally, though rarely, on holidays. We never talked about a god or the Bible at home and, in fact, I don't think I ever heard my parents mention anything biblical except in insults. My most vivid religious memories include being in church on Christmas Eve when the congregation, dressed almost entirely in fur, smelled like scotch. As far as I could tell, most people were only there to socialize, not to pray. Since I had plenty of other social outlets, as well as an emerging sense of progressive feminism, the religious scene as I knew it was definitely not for me.

I didn't revisit religion again until graduate school. I studied faith and spirituality from the vantage point of cultural competency as I worked toward a degree in social work. Having left behind my righteous teens and self-absorbed twenties, I was ready to look again at the role of religion in modern life, including my own. This time, however, I was willing to listen to the shared humanity found deep in the stories of faith. And somewhere inside me, buried under years of disdain for religious thought, I felt a slight craving for my own piece of the spiritual life.

Following a near-death experience in a motor vehicle accident, I acted on this craving and sought out a newly formed Unitarian Universalist congregation in Chester Springs, Pennsylvania, called WellSprings. Knowing something of the UU Principles, I expected to find a community of fellow social justice advocates who would likely tolerate my ambivalent views on religion. What I did not know was how profoundly this community would affect my understanding and acceptance of my brother's recovery process and, ultimately, my own spiritual practice.

I joined one of WellSprings's "small groups" as a way to get to know people and learn more about the community. Designed to enhance spiritual development, small groups meet weekly for ten weeks and offer an opportunity to engage with spiritual content in a close group setting. I came to the first meeting with the expectant angst of a religious outsider and a well-planned exit strategy in case I needed to escape. I knew that no one would doubt my story if I said that an evening meeting was just too much for me. I was still recovering from the car accident, after all. But I stayed. I quickly realized that my longing to know more about the group members' relationships with god-like things was greater than my apprehension.

Our Wednesday night discussions about spirituality stemmed from a collective interest in human wellness, not from a common understanding about the source of divinity. In fact, the only thing we agreed on was that this source was ultimately beyond definition, and, as such, necessarily excluded no one. I was a valid member of a spiritual group despite my revelation of skepticism. This was a gift that I had neither sought nor anticipated. But perhaps even more significantly, I came to terms with how much I had been struggling with my brother's fearless acceptance of a Higher Power. For the past several months I had been wondering how this most beloved person in my life had found grace in something I had been so reluctant to even explore. And what did this mean for him, for me, and for our relationship?

These questions seemed most pressing the day my brother shared the list of fears and resentments he had developed as a result of taking the Fourth Step's fearless moral inventory.

I was astounded. Truly fearless in nature, his list revealed a self-reflective courageousness that I did not know he possessed— and that I longed to have myself. His connection to this Higher Power had allowed him the space and safety to consider dark elements of his experience.

I was called to task. Where did I stand? Did I have the strength to take my own inventory?

My small group at Wellsprings had become a place where, for the first time in my life, I could talk openly about both my skepticism and my fear of dogmatic religion. The group encouraged me to explore these feelings fully, especially as they related to my spiritual life. It became clear during the meetings that a carefully constructed fear-based wall stood in the way of my spiritual development—a fear that I ultimately wouldn't be accepted into a faith community once my doubts were revealed, a fear that had distanced me from my beloved brother's recovery process.

Slowly, the wall came down. In a reflection at the end of our meeting on October 8, 2008, I wrote,

> I am proud of myself for being so honest with this group. Talking today was instrumental in allowing me the space and time to process my struggle with my spiritual development—what "spiritual" means to me and what I still have to learn. I am so glad to be here. I feel a part of something larger than myself for the first time in my life. How truly gracious.

And so, I began my own inventory.

The timing of my brother's participation in AA and my accident, which provoked my search for a spiritual home, often leaves me wondering about the nature of coincidence. Before my experience with Unitarian Universalism, I would not have believed that our lives had purposely collided in this way in order to teach me something. And while I still do not believe that harmful things such as my accident are purposeful, I do believe that the ever-presence of the spiritual world is instructive. It has taught me to embrace this coincidence and celebrate how it gave me an opportunity to develop and cherish my spiritual life.

Step Five

Admitted to God, to ourselves, and to another human being the exact nature of our wrongs.

O Amazing Grace, I once was blind and now I (am starting to) see.

And I am willing to be seen.

I am willing to stop playing hide and no seek with life, but instead, when my name is called for,

To respond, "Here I am."

Quaking maybe, unsteady maybe, but "Here I am."

I am willing to be seen by the eyes most available and nearest to me: my own and those of someone I trust.

I am willing to be held and to behold a gaze of love that offers a free and forgiving way.

As free and as forgiving as I am willing to be seen.

Amen.

Admitting to God and Self

Chris

I did not think I would be doing the Fifth Step on my birthday. Of course, at one point I did not think a birthday without booze could be a fun time. I am a recovering alcoholic. I am a Unitarian Universalist. Among the many identities I claim, these two complement and challenge each other. Each has its own path to realization, and now, for me, those paths are joined.

I procrastinated doing my Fifth Step because I had procrastinated doing my Fourth Step (taking moral inventory of my life). I had heard people talk about how difficult doing the Fourth and Fifth Steps was and it gave me pause. On the other hand, I also had heard about people who did only Steps One, Two, and Three and did not stay sober, which gave me some incentive to do the "action steps." My Alcoholics Anonymous sponsor did not badger me to get it done. My sponsor is my sponsor for that reason, having a balanced style of guidance without too much pressure and just enough nudging to keep me growing in my sobriety. We set a deadline to do the Fifth Step on my belly-button birthday, which was shortly before my AA birthday.

As with many things in life, I had made the Fifth Step into something much bigger and more dramatic than it turned out to be. I tend to work myself up, get all anxious over doing something just right, wanting to do it as perfectly as possible. The more I psyche myself up over something, the less inclined I am to do it, lest I fall short of perfection. Why do today what I can put off till tomorrow?

Not only did my procrastination inhibit doing the work of Step Five, but the kind of soul-searching and soul-*sharing* it entails was not the sort of thing I was inclined to do. I was guarded in my thoughts and feelings, showing only what I wanted people to see. I'm not sure how I came to be like that. I feel quite blessed to have been raised in a loving and affectionate home. Perhaps the dominant culture itself has inhibited me from sharing in an authentic, deep, vulnerable way with even my closest friends and family. Whatever the reason, sharing my feelings, let alone my "wrongs," was a challenge. As an active alcoholic, I certainly committed more than my fair share of wrongs, although my path to alcoholism began in much the same way as those whose consumption of alcohol would be labeled "normal."

I drank my first real drink as a young teenager. I say "real" drink because prior to that, I had had only the tiniest tastes when my father would have a beer with dinner (which was rare, because there was hardly ever alcohol in our house). I would eagerly ask for a sip, because surely something forbidden must taste magical. It was not the exotic potion I imagined it to be. Nevertheless, in my later teen years and into young adulthood, I acquired the taste for beer—along with many other alcoholic beverages.

Without sharing the tragic details of the many alcohol-induced adventures I experienced—some of which I know only by hearing them recounted by those who witnessed them—my drinking habit got progressively worse. It caused me to do dumber and dumber things until it seemed that the only dumb things left to do were to seriously injure myself or others, get arrested, or die.

About a year before hitting bottom, I discovered Unitarian Universalism. In a way, my path to Unitarian Universalism began earlier in my life through a series of partly connected experiences. Growing up, my first faith community was a liberal Christian church, which I drifted away from as a teenager. As a young adult, I made a brief sojourn into a nondenominational evangelical Christian community, again followed by a time of church abstinence. These two different experiences addressed the same innate calling to some kind of spiritual activity—a calling I would respond to later in life.

In the progressive liberal Christian community, a mentor challenged me to seek out and practice an authentic faith. Later, as I studied world religions, I was struck by the similarity of certain fundamental tenets of those traditions. I found a potential spiritual home and way of life when I attended a Unitarian Universalist church located in a conservative community. Since then my faith has deepened, and my participation in Unitarian Universalism has grown.

The synergy of my recovery from alcoholism and my faith in Unitarian Universalism is revealed in the Fifth Step: to admit to God, to myself, and to another human being the exact nature of my wrongs. Identifying my wrongs took place during the Fourth Step: making a searching and fearless moral inventory of myself. In looking at people, places, and things that had affected me, and my role in those experiences, I could identify my character defects in the wrongs I had committed.

The second Principle of Unitarian Universalism states that "we affirm and promote justice, equity, and compassion in human relations." As an active alcoholic, I did not promote justice, equity, and compassion in human relations with many of my friends, family, and coworkers. Moreover, my addiction resulted in behaviors that did not, as the first Principle states, "affirm and promote the inherent worth and dignity of every person"—neither my own nor others.

The concept of self-worth has often perplexed me. Through my experience in Unitarian Universalism, I am cultivating a new sense of self-worth, in which admitting my wrongs to God, myself, and another human being is allowed and even encouraged. This kind of "confession" is not the same as admitting that I have no worth and dignity because of those wrongs.

In doing the Fifth Step—which is more than just thinking, writing, and speaking my wrongs to myself, but also speaking them aloud to another person—I could unlink my behavior from my being. In other words, my past behavior need not define who I was, am, and could be. This is where the first Principle of Unitarian Universalism is so applicable: the inherent worth and dignity of every person. While my behavior did not always reflect my worth and dignity, I embodied them nonetheless. I had worth and dignity even when I did not believe it myself. I had worth and dignity, not because it was something I could earn, but I had it by virtue of being alive and being a part of an interdependent web of existence that also has worth and dignity. A person's worth and dignity is inherent because it is given and received by grace, and there is nothing a person can do or not do that can add to or subtract from their worth and dignity.

I needed to hear that particular message of Unitarian Universalism and perform an exercise like the Fifth Step in order to clarify the distinction between my being and my behavior. I needed to learn it because it was not taught to me, neither in secular society nor in my original religious communities. Whereas the forms of Christianity I experienced taught me that I am a "fallen" human, a sinner, and that only through Jesus Christ can I be redeemed, Unitarian Universalism teaches that I am worthy already. Whereas the dominant culture taught me that self-worth is an external commodity to be earned and acquired—via academic achievement, athletic prowess, looking a certain way, wearing certain clothes—Unitarian Universalism teaches that I am worthy already.

I now realize that I was neither the first nor the last person to exhibit such character defects and commit such wrongs. They are shortcomings with which anyone can identify and behaviors demonstrated by both sober and drunk people. Thus, the first Principle of Unitarian Universalism and the Fifth Step of AA are a good match for any who are willing to accept them. As Unitarian Universalists, we can admit to God, god, Goddess, goddess,

Nature, the mystery, the divine—whatever we choose to call that which is greater than ourselves—and admit to ourselves and to another human being the exact nature of our wrongs. We can reaffirm our inherent worth and dignity and live in greater wholeness with ourselves, humanity, and the universe.

Exact Nature of My Wrongs

Rosemary

It's hard to say which is harder: facing God or facing yourself. I knew I was an alcoholic after one too many drunken sprees in the middle of the night, one too many hangovers I could not medicate away, one too many night terrors from which my long-recovering husband could not awaken me. I knew I was an alcoholic when I sat hunched over my computer, glass of scotch in hand, trying to write a sermon I could not feel, making no sense to myself. I knew I was an alcoholic when I preached from my pulpit about free faith and the love of God, and felt neither loved nor free.

The first three steps for me took only a few weeks; my Fourth and Fifth Steps took two years. I couldn't make lists of my resentments fast enough: condescending congregants, belligerent relatives, nearly anybody who didn't see the world the way I did. But I couldn't detail any of it without the help of a grid. I had so much shame and disappointment in myself that I literally could not find the words. Thankfully, the Big Book supplied the words for me, as I filled out a worksheet I found on a Fifth-Step website, following directions supplied by the Big Book.

Ministry itself was a major part of my shame. It was a second career for me, one I had undertaken after being surprised by God and her call for me. I knew the very language that I used was antithetical to parts of the liberal tradition that best expressed my faith. It took almost a decade of discernment before I felt confident enough to prepare for the assignment, and even as I started, I kept wondering why God would seek me out. Over time, I came to view this understanding of myself as an extraordinary privilege, the process itself best expressed by a seminary colleague who told me, "God does not call the qualified; God qualifies the called."

But the disease of alcoholism that overtook me after decades of "civilian" drinking seemed, above everything else, a betrayal of God's gift to me. My mistreatment of that gift, my failure to protect the trust the Holy and others had placed in me was the most bitter, most painful aspect of my struggle to recover. I could not bring myself to talk about it with myself, much less talk about it with God. The shame was paralyzing—shame about things I had done or failed to do, even deeper shame that often I could not remember what I had done or failed to do.

While I still drank, the disappointed, belittling, and accusatory voices of congregants, colleagues, and friends caused hardly a ripple in my consciousness. But as I got sober, the pink cloud faded, and the wreckage of my past (and my present) became clear, those voices amplified in my mind. They articulated what I came to believe God must really think of me: that I was a hypocrite, a failure, unworthy of trust or confidence. Sobriety brought me clarity about what my drinking had cost me, and I was not at all sure I could ever earn it back.

I said as much at a meeting one morning in the early months of my sobriety, when I openly despaired of ever feeling worthy again. As we ended the meeting with the Serenity Prayer, a woman I didn't know told me that if I kept coming to meetings, if I kept sober, I would one day see returned to me everything I believed I had lost. By that time, I had been coming to meetings enough to believe the truth of her words in material terms. But what could meetings do to restore to me the rightness of my call? And how could the Fifth Step do anything for me except hurt me more than I had already hurt myself?

I did what any self-respecting alcoholic in early sobriety would do: I stalled. It didn't help that my first sponsor, a committed woman who (still) eats, sleeps, and lives the program, felt judgmental to me. She was never really unkind, and she gave freely of her time and wisdom. Without her, I might never have made it through the first year. But she felt too perfect, too redeemed to be a good listener to my lengthy chronicles of behavior unbecoming a woman who had dedicated her life to things of the Spirit.

Eventually, that same woman "fired" me as a sponsee, ostensibly because I didn't call her every day. Of course, my tortured brain simply added her and her behavior to my growing list of resentments. As I continued to attend meetings, as I kept talking to friends and sharing my struggles in the congregation and in life, it became increasingly clear that I very much needed to move on to my Fifth Step. Without a sponsor for the time being, I had no one with whom I could overreact when I considered how little progress I was making in my recovery. The same overachieving tendency that made me dissatisfied in other areas of my life emerged in my recovery. And as if that were not enough, a good friend in the program simply asked me, "Don't you want to be free?"

Freedom became in that moment a magic word. It was an ideal I had been pursuing my entire life. Sharing my story would help me to secure my freedom, and although I knew I could tell it to any trusted person, even my therapist, I also knew that it made sense to find a sponsor who could walk with me for this next leg of my journey. I stumbled a few times in my search: I found an authoritarian woman whose questions only enhanced my shame, then another woman with great recovery who turned out to be even busier than me. One day, however, I went to a new meeting, in despair about an impending meeting with my (at the time) very punitive board of trustees at the congregation. I was so distraught that I took part in the "burning desire"—a portion of many meetings reserved for those who believe their sobriety to be in jeopardy. I wasn't sure I would head for the nearest bar, but the truth was, I didn't know what I might do. I only knew I didn't want to drink again.

I found a lot of hope and help at that meeting. Even more importantly, I found my new sponsor. Ellen (not her real name) worked in the world of theater. Warm and kind, single and child-free, she lived a life that was, in some ways, a marked contrast to mine. Yet listening to her talk about her life and sobriety, I envied her sense of balance. In the language of the rooms, she had what I wanted. So I went up to her after the meeting and asked if she would consider being at least my temporary sponsor. My request seemed to delight her, and we agreed to talk it over at lunch the following week. As I got to know her, I felt good about following my hunch to just ask her. Ellen was busy living her life, but she put sobriety first. We both saw ourselves as driven, creative people who judged ourselves harshly, yet Ellen seemed to have found a way out of the shame and judgment that consumed a big part of my life.

It wasn't long before our temporary arrangement became permanent, and it was Ellen who listened to my Fifth Step one sunny afternoon in a nearly empty open-air plaza near my church. By the time I met her there, we had prayed together, gone to meetings together, told each other about some of our triggers and the people, places, and things that could put us in jeopardy. There at a steel table, I opened my three-ring binder and read to her the details of all the worst behaviors of my life that I could remember. Her only response was one of deep empathy and compassion. She had a non-anxious presence to which I aspired constantly in my work. Best of all, her kindness helped to restore for me the love of God that I knew intellectually but had been unable to feel for a long time.

Ellen reminded me that the fearless moral inventory I had worked on with such fear and loathing was not meant to be a catalogue of horror stories but a record of a complex human life, damaged by alcoholism but not destroyed. That record held many mistakes, but it also held faithful work, integrity, kindness, and love for others and for the God of my understanding. When we were done, she hugged me and reminded me of what the Big Book recommends: that we take quiet time alone, thanking God for the chance to know God better. I had planned to sit quietly in the sanctuary of another church, but by the time we were done, the ones nearby were closed. So I rode the bus home, in the solitude unique to crowded cities, and felt the shame of the past several years gradually fading away. I was no longer a hypocrite after all. I could speak again of the love that holds us all and not feel outside of that love.

As hard as it is for liberal religious people to admit, we know when we have missed the mark—we just won't call it sin. But it eats at us just the same, until we face the ways we have fallen short, until we are ready to try again, knowing we will always be welcomed by God with open arms and an open heart. Having faced my shortcomings, I can be of service now, in ways beyond my ministry, but also deeply connected to it. I am not yet all that I hope to be, but I am so much more than I was. I feel fortunate; best of all, each day, I feel more free.

Step Six

Were entirely ready to have God remove
all these defects of character.

Spirit of Sobriety, God of my Understanding,
As I look back on my life, I see the places where I have
been selfish and self-absorbed; where I have lied to
myself or to others;
where I have sought after my own gain;
where I have been afraid and that fear has ruled my
life.
What a burden these faults have placed upon me!
How weary I have become!
I am so ready to lay these faults down for the greater
hope of being restored to sanity;
for the possibility of a new life no longer moored to the
past.
Oh Spirit of Life,
Help me to step into this new future and to take this
Sixth Step now.
(silence for a time)
Amen.

Entirely Ready for Defects

Celeste

"Defects of character? What defects of character?" I asked my sponsor shortly before starting the Sixth Step. "If you can't find any," she said, "then you've probably got to go back to the Fourth Step—to make a searching and fearless moral inventory. You will surely find them there." As a Unitarian Universalist, I had bought into my own interpretation of the Universalist side of my faith tradition—that I was born with inherent worth and dignity and that because I was basically good instead of depraved, I had nothing to repent. I now understand that the first Principle—"we covenant to affirm and promote the inherent worth and dignity of every person"—is both deeply meaningful and spiritually flawed. While it affirms human worth and dignity, it does not provide a way to grapple with the times when my willfulness leads me to diminish my own dignity. The Sixth Step acknowledges that part of being human is to have defects of character.

Before engaging with the Sixth Step, I naively believed that my inherent goodness was a protection against what AA calls "character defects." Fortunately, my journey into sobriety has led me toward a deeper understanding of what it means to be a perfectly imperfect human being who must regularly reflect on my own character defects. By practicing the Sixth Step, I've also learned how powerful it is to ask God to remove these defects.

I quit drinking on August 27, 2005, after nearly twenty years of struggling with whether or not I was an alcoholic. I had realized about ten years before that my drinking had become a concern, but I could hide it pretty well. Or so I thought. I looked at others who claimed to be in recovery as weak and worthy of my pity. I did not see myself in their story. Now, facing the Sixth Step, I saw being labeled an alcoholic as the biggest defect of character—and the biggest shame I could imagine. I believed that if anyone else knew my secret struggles with self-doubt, if my imperfections were discovered and then possibly exploited, and all my character defects laid bare, I would no longer be able to be a minister and do the work that I loved. I was afraid that if I confronted my character defects in a direct and forthright way, the full awareness of them would crush something precious, innocent, and almost childlike within me. So when I balked at taking this seemingly simple step, my sponsor encouraged me to acknowledge my resistance.

I brought all of these worries and fears to the Sixth Step. My first reaction was to pick it apart intellectually. "First, what does it mean to be entirely ready?" I asked my sponsor. "How can you be entirely ready for anything?" I continued my rant: "And what about God? I don't believe in a God that removes my shortcomings any more than I believe in a God that could stop tsunamis or that interferes in history." My sponsor listened to me with infinite patience. Finally I argued about defects of character. "Isn't this just another Calvinistic attempt to make me feel like a lowly worm?" I explained to her that I was a Unitarian Universalist, who believed in the inherent worth and dignity of all persons, including my own. What was this business about character defects?

She pointed to chapter five in the Big Book of Alcoholics Anonymous, and we looked at what constituted character defects. She had me write them down. Character defect #1: perfectionism. OUCH. I kept drinking because I believed it helped me to maintain an image of perfection. I had to be the perfect minister and the perfect pastoral caregiver; I had to give perfect sermons. In fact, drinking and sermon writing went hand in hand, because I believed somehow that drinking would allow the creative muse to fully emerge, thereby making the sermons more—well, more perfect. In sobriety, I learned I didn't have to be perfect. I just had to be me—and stay sober.

Character defect #2: arrogance. Facing up to my own arrogance was hard, because I liked to think of myself as a humble person. But the truth is that I believe I am right and that if people did things my way, the world would be a better place. Underlying the character defect of arrogance is resentment, because when things don't go my way, I resent having to bend or change to accommodate others. I spent plenty of nights sitting at my desk, stewing over the times when my suggestions or ideas weren't immediately received with great rejoicing. Drinking fueled my overinflated ego and sense of self. It was the reassurance I thought I needed.

The list was growing longer! I explored envy, my sense of entitlement, and my religious arrogance. I came to understand that feelings of superiority and inferiority were one and the same. I realized that having character defects simply makes me human—no more, no less. The Twelve Steps differ from the Unitarian Universalist seven Principles in their expectation of *doing something* with the realization that we are all both perfect and flawed, and that addressing our character defects is a lifelong spiritual practice.

The Sixth Step asks us if we are now ready to let God remove from us all the things that we have admitted are objectionable. Who or what, then, was this God who was going to remove these character defects? Did this God have a magic wand with which to wave away all my personality flaws? I realized that my concept of God was too simplistic. I had to find another understanding of God if I was to seriously engage with this Step.

I had long since abandoned the notion of God as Big Daddy in the Sky that so many of us learn about in childhood. What then, if anything, would take His place? I'm willing to admit that God may not exist as an outside force, that God may be a figment of my imagination. Yet this God whom I have come to understand as Universal Love is very real to me. It has become more than just a Big Idea; it has become a real Presence that constantly beckons me to my highest self. It holds the plumb line against my character defects, and lovingly reminds me when I am leaning too far away from the most conscious person I can be. Do I believe in a God who has supernatural powers? No—that concept of God has no meaning for me. Do I believe in a God who walks with me daily, who provides me with a vision of the best that human life can be? Yes. That's the God I listen to, and pray to, daily.

As I wrestled with this Sixth Step, I recalled the time that I stepped on a needle, and it drove itself deep into my heel. I tried everything to get it out, including some self-rigged magnets and other, ultimately futile attempts. Despite my best efforts, I finally had to realize that I could not remove the needle by myself and had to consign myself to surgery. I needed help. Because I have a relationship with God, I am comfortable turning some things over to Him/Her. I don't know how the surgeon removed that needle, and it didn't matter to me. I put myself in his capable hands and awoke to discover that the pain was gone and so was the needle. As I engaged with Step Six, I realized that the part that *I* could do was to get ready—to prepare; the part that God did was to remove my shame about having character defects at all.

This brings me to the first part of Step Six, "to be entirely ready." What would it mean, I wondered, to be entirely ready to have my character defects removed? As I continued to pray about this Step, I remembered the time I went skydiving. I had a dive instructor strapped on my back. As we crouched on the edge of the plane, the dive instructor asked, "Are you ready to skydive?" I had to answer in the affirmative, completely, with no reservations, because once I jumped out of that plane, there was no crawling back. I either said yes with my whole heart and conviction, or I did not jump. After much prayer and meditation, I realized that being entirely ready to have God remove defects of character did not mean that I believed I would then be perfect. I would *always* have character defects. However, it did mean that I finally had the courage to face those defects, to name them, and to jump into that space that I knew as God—a loving, real Presence whose only desire for me was to live a life of integrity, grace, and service.

The Sixth Step is not an action item but a spiritual practice. Although I had already decided not to drink anymore, I came to realize that being "entirely ready to have God remove all these defects of character" was perhaps more difficult than quitting alcohol itself. Being entirely ready is like the moment you say yes to a proposal of marriage or lifelong partnership; it's when your heart says yes to a new vocational opportunity you've been preparing for; it's like saying yes to the adoption agent who asks if you're ready for the new baby in your life; and it's like saying yes to that skydive instructor, before you free-fall into space, knowing that you will be caught and carried by forces you did not create and cannot control. It is saying yes to a Spirit of Life that loves us—character defects and all.

All My Relations

Walks With Shield (Lakota)

I recently celebrated twenty-two years of sobriety, and time has flown by. As an American Indian and a member of the Oglala Sioux Tribe, my sobriety date has special meaning. My first day sober was June 25, 1990, the anniversary of the Battle of Little Big Horn. After sobering up, I learned that my great grandmother, Lizzy Horse Woman, had lived through this historic battle in which my Lakota (Sioux) ancestors and their Cheyenne relatives defeated George Armstrong Custer and the US Seventh Calvary. That battle changed their lives in a profound way. Similarly, that day changed my life in a profound way, as I emerged from an almost fatal battle with alcoholism and embarked on a Twelve-Step program of recovery and a new life replete with blessings and opportunity.

Each step of recovery within the Twelve Steps of Alcoholics Anonymous has been an opportunity for growth and reflection, and has challenged me to the core of my being. Since the Sixth Step suggests that I have defects of character, it prompts me to consider my concept of self. The idea of readiness is also important because life continually necessitates change. There are times when I feel uncertain about or averse to change, but I have learned everything in life continually changes, and my ability to adapt to that change is key.

The issue of whether we have defects of character remains debatable, but certainly no one knows whether this is true. Rather, it is a matter of belief. On the one hand, my concept of an ideal character would be to embody only positive traits. However, as a human being I will at times exhibit traits that may cause harm or reflect my self-centeredness. It is easy to see why these traits could be called defects; to me, this language simply highlights that they are important areas to work on. I found many of them in my searching and fearless moral inventory. I have also viewed my character as having traits that are commensurate with my abilities. I have the ability to be selfish, I have the ability to procrastinate, I have the ability to lie, and so on. As many of us in AA continue to take an inventory of ourselves, as written in the Tenth Step, we realize that there are aspects of our character that we perceive as needing improvement. Indeed, when we work on them and make efforts toward growth, we begin to see change, often profound change.

The Sixth Step refers to being ready to have God remove the defects. In earlier steps, we established our own understanding of God. Central to that understanding is that this God is a power greater than ourselves. This simply means, in the broadest sense, that as human beings, we never have all the power. When we open ourselves to the idea that there is power greater than ourselves, we place ourselves in the best position to facilitate our growth, development, and recovery.

The concept of power has great relevance to the Sixth Step. As I look back at the path my life has taken, I can only conclude that great power has been working in my life. I was adopted at the age of five months and grew up as a beloved child in a Unitarian Universalist church. My parents were Anglo and raised me in a loving tradition. I liked the Unitarian Universalism because it never made me claim one conception of God. Rather, it introduced me to many beliefs and still does to this day. During the 1970s, when I was about thirteen years old, I got involved with alcohol and drugs. All I wanted to do was have fun, but many difficult consequences followed. I had no understanding of what was happening to me, but it always seemed like the real me had to deal with the consequences. It was terrifying to come out of a blackout and be locked up in jail or strapped down to a hospital bed. I became progressively more isolated and stopped interacting with positive people because I had no idea what was going on. However, when people confronted me about my drinking, or I found myself in a situation that required me to answer for what happened, I was at a loss. I felt awful, so I tried to avoid looking at the reality of my situation.

My introduction to AA opened my eyes as I began to assess where I was in life. The meetings helped me to learn about the program, and the friends and sponsors I acquired taught me about what is important in life and how to stay sober. I began to pray to a vague conceptualization of a Higher Power. Being an American Indian shaped my initial concept of God or the Creator. I found it unnecessary to extensively describe God. I said prayers and then eventually started to meditate. In the beginning I prayed for strength: strength to stay sober, strength to be guided, and strength to grow and make positive changes. I enrolled in school, and years later obtained a position as a registered nurse within a government agency. I was asked to work on a Native American program, and it was then I decided that I needed to know exactly what tribe I was from. I knew my birth certificate said Sioux, but I also knew that Sioux includes several tribes of American Indians from the Great Plains region of the United States. I decided to say a prayer to find my birth mother, concluding that she would be able to inform me about my lineage. I also knew in practical terms that she might not be alive, could be addicted to drugs, or could have any number of circumstances that would prevent me from connecting with her. However, I felt ready for anything. Naturally, I always had some curiosity about who she was, but I had never taken any sustained action other than obtaining my original birth certificate and some adoption records. So I said the prayer, and after praying, I felt centered and was certain it was the right thing to do.

Shortly thereafter, I found myself in Salt Lake City, Utah, at a government conference with many American Indians and Alaska Natives in attendance. My new position in government was exciting, and I was learning a great deal. I noticed a man sitting at the end of the table wearing a green beret with a Purple Heart on it. He had an eagle feather tied to his beret. I happened to speak with him during the break and learned that he was from the Pine Ridge Indian Reservation in South Dakota. My adoption records identified my birth mother as being from that reservation. I told him the story, and he said it might be possible to find her, so immediately I felt optimistic and excited at this prospect. We ended up going to lunch, and I learned that he was a Vietnam combat veteran, injured during the war after being shot down in a helicopter.

That night, our conference attended an Inipi ceremony, or Sweat Lodge, as many people refer to it. I learned it was a purification ceremony and one of the seven sacred Lakota ceremonies. My new friend asked if he could ride with my group, so we planned to meet beforehand at my hotel room. Upon arrival, he informed me that he had called his mother on Pine Ridge and found out we had the same grandmother! When he told me, a feeling of electricity ran through my body, and I could feel my entire being focus on what he was telling me. Later, I found out that this man was my brother in the Lakota way, but in the way of the Western world, he would be considered my cousin. That night in the Sweat Lodge with him and others was a profound spiritual experience that affirmed my journey to reconnect with my lineage.

Shortly after that momentous conference, my brother informed me that he had acquired my birth mother's phone number. As I dialed the number, I once again felt the electricity of anticipation coursing through my being. When she answered, I said my name and my date of birth and that my journey to find my birth mother had led me to her. About a month later, I found myself in South Dakota, knocking on her front door. When she opened the door, I faced a woman I looked like. Her warm smile greeted me as I entered her household. This was the beginning of a wonderful relationship that continues to this day. Learning so much about my Lakota family and our traditions has impacted my career trajectory in positive ways. I will always be grateful to my brother. His legacy of spiritual growth and of helping others embodies that of a Lakota warrior.

When I told my adoptive parents about all these events, I wanted to be sensitive to them and considerate of their feelings. My father said to me, "I used to lay awake at night and worry how I would tell your mother you had been killed." That was the trajectory I was on as a young man out drinking and driving; my life was in peril.

This is the context in which I reflect upon my readiness for change as it relates to the Sixth Step. When I remain aware of that and my relationship to the Wakan Tanka (Creator, as I understand Him), I find new growth and revelations, which strengthen the journey of my spirit, mind, and body. This is what the Sixth Step and the other steps of Alcoholics Anonymous mean to me: that recovery is possible.

In the words of the Lakota, *Mitakuye oyasin, ho hecetu yelo, wopila tanka, aho* ("All my relations, it is so, thank you, amen.").

Step Seven

Humbly asked Him to remove
our shortcomings.

Spirit of Life, may I be done with making demands.
My ransom notes have profited me not at all.
"Deliver me this windfall at this time, at this place,
  exactly of my choosing! . . . Or else!"
The ransom demands put my own soul up for sale.
And very cheaply.
So now I ask:
May I? If it is your will and it is the appointed time . . .
May I . . . know love, know peace and know grace?
And may this love, peace, and grace—being not mine
  to borrow or steal, but yours to share—find a home
  in my heart.
Amen.

Humbly Ask

Josie

The journey through the Seventh Step has been about learning to accept all of my imperfections as I build a trusting relationship with a power greater than myself. I have come to believe that this power works in my life not by transforming me into a better person but by providing the connection that enables me to tap into all the good qualities that are already there.

When I first entered recovery over twenty years ago, I would not have described myself as spiritually deficient. Sure, I was overweight, but I had a good job, a loving family, and a strong faith. My problem was that I couldn't seem to stop overeating and that I was unhappy with the resulting weight gain and general feeling of being unattractive.

The benefits of hindsight and the contrast of life in recovery have shown me that my issues with food and weight were just the surface issues. My job paid well and made my loved ones proud of me, but I didn't enjoy it. My family loved me, but too often when they expressed confidence in me, I felt that it was undeserved and that they didn't really understand me. When they criticized me, I felt unacceptable, and their words reinforced my low opinion of myself. I understand today why they often seemed so frustrated with me. I suffered deeply from a lack of self-esteem and a belief that life would really start when I finally got my act together.

I did have what I considered to be a strong faith at the time. I believed God loved me unconditionally, but it was nothing like the connection I feel today. I grew up in a religion that taught me to believe certain truths. I was encouraged to question, but only to the extent that those questions led me back to the teachings of the church. Increasingly, I was becoming aware that my own values were often in conflict with those teachings. I alternated between feeling guilty about my values and feeling angry with the church.

I entered recovery, in part, because I wanted to find a way to accept myself the way I am. I thought I would learn to be "fat and happy." I learned that I had an addiction to food that, while chronic, could be arrested one day at a time. My early recovery focused a lot on learning to abstain from compulsive overeating and to deal with the feelings, some pleasant, some uncomfortable, that came with shedding and keeping off unwanted pounds. The first time I went through the Steps with a sponsor, I don't remember feeling much of anything about Step Seven. I said the prayer and moved on to Step Eight.

As I look back, I notice the impulse to pass judgment on my shallow way of working my recovery. But my recovery has moved forward by degrees. In the beginning, I was so grateful to finally be in a healthy-sized body. I had tried to lose weight unsuccessfully for years. Accepting that I was an addict and asking for help, from the group and from my Higher Power, was working. I was in recovery. I was making new connections. It was enough, in the beginning. But after several years, I found myself craving something more.

At this point, my career was taking off. I had a loving husband and two beautiful daughters, and had been maintaining a healthy weight for several years. What else could I possibly want? I wanted a deeper connection. I found a new sponsor and began working the Twelve Steps in earnest. When I got to Step Seven, I was struck by the fact that although I had been in the program for several years it seemed like I was hearing this Step for the first time. I started to understand it differently. I realized that real recovery involved changing my life and not just my eating habits. I knew that a Higher Power had helped me to abstain from compulsive overeating, so it made sense that any real, lasting changes in my behavior would involve depending on a Higher Power as well.

For me, the most glaring example of behavior that needed to change was my tendency to procrastinate. I found that I couldn't just ask God to remove this defect and expect my life to be forever changed. Step Seven wasn't a onetime plea, but a constant process of asking God to help me change. This process was filled with much frustration. I would ask God to remove my procrastination and then catch myself avoiding important tasks, particularly at work. I thought that clearly I wasn't working Step Seven right because I was still procrastinating.

I found myself going through the motions in many key areas of my life. I continued to follow the religion of my childhood because it was easier than making a change. I spent many years trying to make it work, trying to be the person people expected me to be. I knew lots of people who could dutifully go to church each week and appreciate the things that resonated with them while ignoring the ones that didn't. I'm not sure why it was so difficult for me, but I think it had something to do with my growing connection to the God of my understanding. I became aware of the inauthenticity of professing to believe in something I doubted and aligning myself with an institution that was at odds with some of my core values. These were some of the shortcomings that Step Seven talks about.

Leaving the church of my childhood was one of the most difficult things I'd ever done. It tested my marriage and disappointed many very important people in my life. It also gave me a sense of freedom and peace that I had never known. I learned that honoring the connection I feel to whatever this power is that is greater than myself is essential to my continued growth and recovery.

I have learned through both my Twelve-Step experiences and my Unitarian Universalist faith to question the role of a Higher Power in my life. In the context of the religion of my childhood, my questioning felt like a crisis of faith. Since becoming a UU, I question more than ever, but I no longer feel like I'm in crisis. My Higher Power doesn't require anything from me but connection. My spiritual growth is about seeking a Higher Power, not about finding one.

In the same way, my continued growth in working the Seventh Step is showing that this Step isn't really about the removal of my defects. I had to learn to let go of expectations about whether or when my defects would be removed. Step Seven is about having the humility to ask God, my Higher Power, for help. My only job is to humbly ask. Sometimes, I do this by identifying a particular defect, like procrastination, and saying a heartfelt prayer. More often, this Step is a state of mind, as is my connection with a Higher Power. First, I accept that there are things about myself, behaviors and attitudes, that I don't like and that get in my way. No matter how long I am in recovery or how much I work the Seventh Step, there will always be imperfections that nag at me. I am human. I am lovable exactly as I am, and I believe that learning to love myself exactly as I am is critical to my continued recovery. In fact, the attitude that excelling is a condition of my worth is one of the defects I humbly ask God to remove.

A voice inside me tells me that my unwanted behaviors and attitudes are, or should be, within my control. Yet they have persisted despite my best efforts. Once I accept these shortcomings, I can acknowledge that I would be better off without them. For me, this is the "humble" part of the Seventh Step. Experience has shown me that connecting with the God of my understanding is a prerequisite for any lasting change. It is through this connectedness that I voice my desire for change. I ask God to remove my defects, but I let go of any expectations about how, when, or whether this will occur.

Some time ago, I pulled out an old list of character defects that I had developed with the help of my sponsor. I had been particularly frustrated with what felt like a lack of progress on the defect of procrastination. While reviewing the list, I was amazed to discover that I had made significant progress on many of the other defects on my list. For example, I am less judgmental and less likely to fall into self-pity than I was when I wrote the list. It was a powerful reminder that I can let go and trust that, as long as I am willing, God will subtly work changes in my life. When I find myself engaging in behaviors I don't like, I try to practice humility. I acknowledge my imperfections and ask for guidance. When I find myself behaving differently and making better choices, I try to practice humility by remembering to be grateful.

I am grateful today. I am grateful for my recovery from addiction, one day at a time. I am grateful for the opportunity to share my experience, strength, and hope with others. I am grateful each time I find that a once-troubling defect isn't troubling me quite so much today. And I am grateful to be learning to be gentle with myself. I don't have to be perfect to feel worthy of love and acceptance.

Humbled by Sobriety

Mark

Every Sunday morning, I walk to a Step Meeting—a meeting that focuses on one of the Twelve Steps of Alcoholics Anonymous—that I attend before going to church. Although I have been in the program for more than seventeen years, I still struggle with discomfort and fear. A particular meeting in March 2009 helped me begin the process of getting through an emotional discomfort. Immediately after the meeting, I wrote about an event that really upset me:

> I came to this meeting in a gloomy mood. I was filled with anxiety, depression, worry, fear, and concern about the financial calamity that has befallen the whole family. The short story is that one of my sons was employed by a person who encouraged the whole family to invest and then stole the money. It has caused deep losses for all of us . . . losses that are going to hurt a lot. As a father, I care so deeply for my children that there are no words to describe the depth of my feelings for them or my desire to take care of them.

And then after church later that day, I wrote these reflections:

> I was reminded again that humility is the answer to many of the issues that face me. I have been very successful with my life. Some of this is due to hard and persistent effort on my part. Some of it is due to luck: my being born at a certain time in the cycle of the world economy that has beneficently smiled on my wife and me.

The first reflection represented the character flaw that brought me down. I always felt that I had to be the best, to do the best, to hold everything together, and to never ask for help. I believed (and was often right) that if I just tried hard enough, I could make happen whatever needed to happen. I took on large projects or responsibilities that consumed my energy and taxed me emotionally. I medicated myself with alcohol, usually after the arduous effort was over.

I struggled for many years with abusive drinking and never let on that it was something I could not control. Each evening, I would say to myself that I would limit my consumption of wine. I would fail, getting buzzed instead. Of course, I would recriminate myself, feel miserable, and then try harder. In the process, I lost a lot of confidence in myself.

Interestingly, I never saw my belief that I was all-powerful and that I *could* do it if I just tried harder as arrogant.

The Big Book states, "As long as we placed our self-reliance first, a genuine reliance upon a Higher Power was out of the question. The basic ingredient of all humility, a desire to seek and do God's will was missing."

I have problems with the "God" part since I don't believe that there is a God. But I do believe that some very wise spiritual perspectives come from the precepts of many religions. As a result, I can seek to do good, to be kind and caring, to work for social justice, and to respect others.

I realized that humility means letting go of the current situation to some degree and trying to understand and embrace its greater meaning and challenge. I could now more easily ask what I am supposed to learn from this. I found my answers through writing and reflecting.

During the meeting, I felt a tiny glimmer of light, a pinhole in the gloom. I better understood the limits of my capacity to fix things, and I recognized that there are larger lessons to be learned here. While I felt clearer, it seemed like I was back in kindergarten, learning all over again what I'd known so well.

I continued to work on the issues for several weeks, and my reflections revealed more about the ways in which my discomfort stemmed from fear. My years in the program prompted some answers.

My initial question to myself was: What am I supposed to understand about my role as a father who fiercely wants to protect and care for his children and their partners, even though I can't assuage their loss? I realized that still more humility is called for and that I should accept my limits and trust in my children's abilities to solve their problems and heal themselves.

This led me to conclude that if I can't fix their problems, maybe I need to revisit the Prayer of St. Francis—often associated with the Eleventh Step. I could try to embrace being an instrument of truth, and to bring as much care, love, and understanding to my children as possible. Thankfully, the program reminds me that I do not have to do this perfectly and that I can strive for progress, not perfection.

A familiar feeling cropped up in the midst of this idea: a fear that I would be seen as abandoning my children. However, I understood that this was the old arrogance: the idea that I should be able to take care of anything and fix everything. This was a major insight for me because I saw how my dis-ease always lurks in the background. I realized that I can let go of some of my need to help beyond my ability to do so.

I am totally convinced that what many in the program call a disease, is for me a chronic dis-ease: an underlying apprehension, sadness, anger, and fear that is always there. I go to meetings to treat those feelings with the love, wisdom, and fellowship of the program. This keeps my dis-ease at bay. I won't be tempted to drink if I continue to work at containing these feelings that might otherwise become stronger. AA helps to keep me emotionally sober.

I also feared that my family might fall apart because of conflict, especially when I heard them occasionally get upset with each other. But I realized that my anxiety and fear about conflict is part of my dis-ease. The antidote is to use the Serenity Prayer to remember what I can and cannot control, and the Prayer of St. Francis to seek to comfort, to love, and to understand rather than to try to take their pain away.

Finally, I thought about how I might gently remind my children that they were responsible for having invested their money in this failed financial scheme. I feared that I might sound cold and callous. Once again, fear dominated my thinking, yet I realized, along with St. Francis, that where there is error I can sow truth, where there are shadows, light. Furthermore, I can do so with love, care, and understanding to the best of my ability. I don't have to avoid having any opinions about what they say about the failed investments.

Once again, I am awed and humbled by the power of this program to help me to understand my humanness in response to life's dilemmas, and when I find myself fearful, to work to heal, a day at a time, using these beautiful Steps.

Step Eight

Made a list of all persons we had harmed, and became willing to make amends to them all.

I have this list in front of me, and it's shocking. I want to avoid this Step; I want to run away, I want to tell myself it wasn't so bad; the damage wasn't that much, they certainly must have forgiven me by now.

That's not what the Step is asking of me. It's asking me to be willing to make amends to them all.

What an order! I can't go through with it. And then, I remember something I heard in the rooms of Recovery, "We claim spiritual progress, not spiritual perfection." If I want to make progress, I must first clear away every excuse I have for not making amends. It's time to come clean. It's time to own up to the damage I've done and the harm I've caused.

In meditation and prayer, I see all those persons I harmed in my mind's eye, and I bless them. I thank them for being one of many teachers on this path. I breathe through the difficulty. I am willing to make amends to them all.

Making the List

Monica

A few years ago, the television show *My Name Is Earl* premiered, and although the last show was taped in 2009, it is still one of my favorite shows to watch. The show centers on Earl, who realizes that his bad luck is the result of the bad things he does to people. He becomes convinced that if he wants a better life, he has to be a better person. So he makes a list of everything bad he has ever done to others, and he commits to doing good deeds, including making amends to those he had wronged in the past.

Earl was not in a Twelve-Step program; however, his act of making a list and his willingness to make amends were vitally important to him developing the humility that would aid him in changing his destructive and harmful behaviors. Humility is foundational to Step Seven, and without humility, the willingness to change and fulfill the requirements in Step Eight—to ask for forgiveness and to forgive oneself and others—will be difficult, if not impossible.

Claiming my seat in Alcoholics Anonymous was the beginning of my spiritual journey. AA is foundational to my life and how I am in the world. Working the Twelve Steps required hard, diligent work, and Unitarian Universalism requires this of me as well.

I stopped using illegal drugs sometime in 1989, and I took my last drink of alcohol on January 7, 1990. As of this writing, I have been sober for more than twenty-two years. I received my preliminary fellowship and ordination into Unitarian Universalist ministry in May 2000. My sobriety and ministry are so closely connected that there is no light between them. I often say that AA and sobriety gave me life, and ministry gives me something to do with my life. Both inspire me to be intentional and vigilant in maintaining a close and intimate connection and relationship with a power greater than myself, that I sometimes call God, Spirit, my Higher Power, or the Source of Life.

The details that follow depend upon my memory because I did not keep the numerous versions of Step-Eight lists I made during my early sobriety. The foundation of my amends list consisted of the people and institutions that I included in the column labeled "I'm resentful at" on my Fourth-Step list. Like sobriety, making my Eighth-Step lists was a process. By the time I reached Step Eight, my tally of people to make amends to had grown to include people and institutions that I did not include on my initial Fourth-Step list. It also included me.

I once heard someone in an AA meeting say, "I would never have allowed someone to treat me the way I treated myself." If someone had done to me some of the things I had done to myself, I would definitely have expected them to make amends to me, and I most likely would not have continued to be their friend. However, I did not hold myself to the same standard regarding how I treated myself. Putting myself on my amends list was not instinctual or intuitive. In fact, had my sponsor not suggested it, I most likely would not have done so. It did not occur to me that the person I hurt most during the years I abused drugs and alcohol was me. The questions and uncertainty that I had to address during this process concerned how much I had limited my potential. For example, in high school and college I frequently participated in basketball practice or games under the influence of drugs or hungover from abusing drugs and/or alcohol. Did I play to my full potential? What opportunities did I miss or ignore because of my addiction? What did my long-term substance abuse do to my brain?

There is so much I do not remember from the twenty-year period of my addiction. Once I accepted that I needed to make amends to myself, the question became, How? How do I make amends for the harm and hurt I caused myself? During the turbulent, chaos-filled days of my early sobriety, two sayings in AA helped me keep perspective and not completely fall into an abyss of hopelessness: "Easy does it" and "Progress and not perfection." With those two phrases bouncing around in my mind, I became willing to forgive myself. Once I was willing, the door opened for me to forgive.

Most of the world's religions and faith traditions profess a belief in the Golden Rule: "Do unto others as you would have them do unto you. Love your neighbor as yourself." My parents used to tell me to treat people the way I wanted to be treated. After twenty-two years of sobriety, most days and in most situations, I am aware that the universe does not revolve around me, so I have added to the Golden Rule: "Treat people the way they want to be treated, which may differ from how I want to be treated." For example, many times I have mistreated my friends by showing up extremely late or not at all to their social gatherings. Sadly, I did not limit this inconsiderate behavior to just my friends. I also missed numerous family gatherings or showed up under the influence of either drugs, alcohol, or both.

To share in-depth about all the people and institutions included on my Eighth-Step lists would take more space than one essay would hold. Therefore, I will only comment on the most important and transformational items. Two of the most important people on my list are my deceased parents. My mother died when I was twenty-two (six years before I got clean and sober), and her death devastated me. Even though I was her primary caregiver from the time she was diagnosed with colon cancer until the day she died, I still had to process and accept the painful memories of the disrespectful and inconsiderate manner in which I had treated her before she got sick. My father died from a heart attack six years later and seven months into my recovery. I will forever be grateful to AA and the Twelve Steps because I was able to tell my father on the day before he died that he was a great dad and that I loved him. Even though I cared for my mother during her terminal illness, and I acknowledged and affirmed my father's parenting, I still had to find a way to make amends to both of them after their deaths. The key to making amends to my parents was to be humble and willing—willing to forgive myself and willing to extend myself to people my parents' ages by spending time with them doing things they enjoyed.

The third-most important item on my overall Eighth-Step list was the US Army. During my sophomore year of college, I joined the Army Reserve Officers' Training Corps. After I graduated with a bachelor degree, I was commissioned as a second lieutenant. However, after nine months on active duty, I received a Less-Than-Honorable Discharge because I failed a drug test. Even though I was aware that I would have to take a drug test when I reported for active duty, I continued to use drugs. Finding a way to make amends to the US government, that invested time and money training me, took me to levels of willingness that I did not think possible. Yet once I became willing, I was nudged toward an opportunity by a friend who suggested that I join the Peace Corps.

Like so many others in the grip of addiction, I had amassed credit card debt. Therefore, another important item on my list was the credit card company. I was well aware that I was at my limit—without the means to make a payment—yet I continued to use the card until I was told to destroy it. I had to be willing to do that and pay off the debt no matter how long it took—which I did.

I have been in recovery for more than twenty-two years and a Unitarian Universalist minister for more than twelve. Working the Twelve Steps of AA and the seven Principles of Unitarian Universalism is foundational to my sobriety and my ministry, because they teach me how to be in relationship with and accountable to myself and others. They also require me to have a relationship with something bigger than myself. For example, the seventh Principle of Unitarian Universalism states, "Respect for the interdependent web of all existence of which we are part." This directly connects to AA's Eighth Step, which invites me back into community and the interdependent web of existence with those I have hurt and caused harm. My AA and UU communities have nurtured me, loved me, and taught me to let my life be my amends. My two beloved communities have also taught me to be mindful that I must treat others the way they want to be treated. Equally important is checking-in with myself each day by asking, Am I treating myself the way I want others to treat me? One of my favorite AA sayings is, "Let it begin with me." It reminds me that if I am humble and am willing to forgive and to ask for forgiveness, my sobriety, my conscious contact with my Higher Power, and my ability to make amends to myself and others are possible in the Ninth Step.

Willing to Make Amends

Geoff

When I was first asked to write about my experience with Step Eight, I responded, "Why can't I get an easier step?" But after further reflection, it seems appropriate to be writing about my experience with this Step during my eighth year of recovery. As with all of the other steps, it has had different meanings over time, so I will share my current understanding.

My spiritual life was basically nonexistent before I entered recovery. I was uncomfortable with any talk of God or a Higher Power. I am forever grateful for the caveat "as we understood Him" being added to the Twelve Steps. Without this simple phrase, I highly doubt that I would be writing these words today. I came into recovery only wanting to escape the pain that my addiction had caused me and those closest to me. I had no concept of any Higher Power and frankly was not all that interested in hearing about it. I was encouraged to do my own investigation and figure out what worked for me.

During a period when I was feeling fairly disconnected from recovery and also looking for a place to take my children so they could have some spiritual roots, I was introduced to a new Unitarian Universalist congregation. I was pleasantly surprised to learn that the minister was in recovery as well, and as we talked, I got the sense that UUs spoke my language. The sense of inclusiveness and spiritual diversity invites many people to enter the door and discover what the spiritual life means for them. This community invited me to take a deeper look at the connection between my recovery and spiritual growth.

From the Twelve Steps and Twelve Traditions book, Step Eight opens with the following:

Steps Eight and Nine are concerned with personal relations. First, we take a look backward and try to discover where we have been at fault; next we make a vigorous attempt to repair the damage we have done; and third, having thus cleaned away the debris of the past, we consider how, with our newfound knowledge of ourselves, we may develop the best possible relations with every human being we know.

Here I will focus on the third and, for me, most challenging part of this process.

The first half of the Eighth Step sounds pretty straightforward: "Made a list of all persons we had harmed." I had a list of people from when I did my Fourth Step, so that was easy. "Became willing to make amends to them all" was a whole other story. There were certain people, such as my stepfather, whom I was fairly sure I wasn't going to be willing to make amends to. I went to Step meetings and heard that I could break down the list into categories: easy amends that I was willing to make now, more difficult amends that I knew I wanted to make but wasn't ready to, and amends that I would never be willing to make. As time goes on, and the first category shrinks as I make amends and grow spiritually, the people in the third category move to the second. I even find myself wishing that my stepfather were still alive so that I could make amends to him in person. It took me many years to realize that the main person I needed to make amends to was the person looking back in the mirror.

While moving into Step Nine, I discovered that making amends to certain people on the list would serve no purpose. This was one of the times early in sobriety that my sponsor was a very good resource. Looking up old girlfriends to make amends seemed like a perfectly good idea as I was struggling with marital problems until I was asked to look at my motivation.

I have found that as time passes, I have naturally become more compassionate, more forgiving and accepting of others' views and opinions. Of course, I am this way when my better self is present, which is by no means all the time. I currently struggle with the line from the Steps and Traditions book, "develop the best possible relations with every human being we know." It's such an easy concept and intellectual exercise, but to actually transform it into a heartfelt experience has been a slow and arduous process for me.

I have the habitual tendency, shared by many who struggle with addictions, to want to isolate from the world and hide. Not only does this keep me from connecting with others, but it keeps me from connecting with myself. One of the biggest amends I have learned to make to myself is to choose a different response when I feel the overwhelming urge to shut down and shut the world out. Simply reaching out to another human being, whether to share how I am feeling or to ask how they are doing, changes everything. The only problem is that at the moments when I most need to do this, I have absolutely no desire to do so. My habit is so ingrained in my cells that before I know it, I have played out the old scenario of hiding from the world and numbing out. Fortunately, now I realize this pattern and I can tell on myself and ask for support from those around me for the next time this happens, which experience tells me will not be long from now.

During my addiction, one of the biggest impediments to developing strong relationships was my constant need to bring the focus back to me. In a conversation, the entire time the other person was talking I would be formulating my response. This would either take the form of offering advice or immediately switching the topic back to me, my life, and my problems. In the AA literature it says that self-centeredness is the root of our troubles. This has definitely been my experience.

One person to whom I needed to make amends was my now ex-wife. She definitely took the brunt of much of my self-centered behavior. I now see how often she tried to put my needs and wants ahead of hers. Early in sobriety, when I was out nearly every night, my sponsor said to me, "Don't you think you should be spending more time home with your wife and kids?" Honestly, that thought rarely, if ever, crossed my mind at that point in my life. I was still wrapped up in what I needed in any given moment. Although we eventually divorced, my ex-wife and I are developing a better relationship now. My need to always be right (and to tell you so) seems to be slipping away. I have heard my former condition described as being an egomaniac with an inferiority complex, which definitely fits the way I used to be.

As I have grown in my spiritual life and recovery, I have gradually learned that the solution is to place my focus on others. This goes against years of habit, and I am by no means perfect at it. I must constantly be reminded that the solution to improving my relationships with others lies in learning how to really be there for them. This means stifling my impulse to try and fix everyone's problems. When I can manage to just listen and truly be present and empathetic, I feel that I am being of service.

It has been a recent transformation for me to turn my entire attention on the other person during a conversation—not formulating a response, coming up with advice, or passing judgment. In this way, I can help whoever is sharing with me connect to their own deeper wisdom, which is where their answers lie. Now I wish that I could do this with all my relationships, instead of only occasionally.

Ironically, these skills are hardest to practice with the people I am closest to. I have no trouble baring my soul in front of a group of strangers, sharing intimate details of how I felt going through personal struggles such as my divorce and getting sober. I also can listen with complete presence to strangers' struggles with their own dark nights of the soul. When it comes to sharing deep emotions with people like my parents and siblings, I feel like I am still in emotional kindergarten.

Today my most sincere wish is that I may become a more fully alive human being, able to stay present for the entire human experience. My mission is to help create a world of peace and service through true presence and authentic connections to others. When I turn toward this and away from my shadow of disconnection and isolation, I feel that I am doing my small part to make this world a better place. Step Eight was the start of developing healthy relationships, as I began to realize how my actions affected other people.

Step Nine

Made direct amends to such people
wherever possible, except when to do
so would injure them or others.

Oh Spirit of Forgiveness, be with me now.
I must make amends for the harm I have caused, but
  I am afraid.
I fear opening old wounds. I fear rejection. I fear
  causing more harm.
And yet, I also know that if I am to fully recover,
  I must acknowledge the wrongs that I have done
  and try to set them right.
Oh Spirit of Love, be with me as I pick up the phone
  and make the call.
Calm me as my hand shakes, my chest tightens, my
  voice feels as though it will die in my throat.
Remind me that to make amends is to build a bridge
  to healing.

Help me to see where an opening may exist, when before there seemed only a dead end.

May I take this step now.

(Silence)

Amen.

The Extravagant Promise

Eric

"Wow. I owe PZ an apology."

It was the first thing that popped into my mind as I woke up. It was a Tuesday, in the spring of 1999. My brother had recently died, and I guess that event had stirred some old memories.

PZ and I had been friends and partners in a couple of reasonably successful casino and dance bands in Philadelphia and New Jersey during most of my heaviest drinking days. It ended badly, in humiliation for me, anger and disgust for him.

I had no idea how to reach him. He had moved, and his old number was no longer in service. I was living in central Pennsylvania and had no connection with anyone from the old days.

I was nine years sober, back to playing trumpet locally with a few bands and enjoying a small amount of success. I had accepted the probability that I wouldn't be playing full-time again and so was able to enjoy such gigs as came my way.

As it happened, I had a gig the following Sunday, some twenty miles from home. I thought nothing of it until I got there and saw that the drummer in the warm-up band was an old drinking buddy from my nights in Atlantic City. After a warm greeting, I casually asked her if she knew what had happened to PZ.

"Yeah, I just saw him last week. He's got this long-term contract at the Taj Mahal. He's been there, like, six years." Then she said something that floored me. "I have his number in my purse."

Okay. I can call that a coincidence.

I called him the next day. In Alcoholics Anonymous, I had been told that there would be times when the opportunity to do a Ninth Step would be presented, and I would know that I needed to act.

PZ was clearly happy to hear from me. He kept repeating, "No! It can't be you. It can't be!" He told me that my now-deceased brother had for a time kept him informed about my bottom (nine months in prison) and my subsequent recovery. When my brother became mortally ill, they lost contact, and PZ had heard nothing since.

After he settled down, I came to the point.

"PZ. The reason I called is that I realized that I owe you an apology for my behavior while we were working together." I had showed up drunk for load-ins, I was hung over for rehearsals and gigs. I had publicly embarrassed him and his business. Being a drunk and a musician is a very public and messy thing. PZ graciously accepted my apologies. His voice was a little shaky when he told me how happy he was that I had given up drinking. He said he hated to see me killing myself that way.

I told him that life was good for me and that I wasn't calling him to "break his stones" for work. I just wanted to apologize.

Nevertheless, he said, "This is too crazy. Just last night we were talking about you. We're putting this thing together. A real show thing. And I was saying that you would be the perfect guy for this. You have exactly the right mind for it."

When I repeated that I wasn't calling for a gig, he said, "Yeah, I get it. But think about it. It'll be huge! It's a Louis Prima tribute. We're doing it as a full-out main-room spectacle. Big band, dancing girls—the whole deal." We were both giant fans of the late Louis.

Well, I thought about it and agreed to do it. We gave it the old college try. As happens so often in show business, some really good ideas just don't work out. We did a lot of hard work, all for naught, but we had a good time trying and we re-established our friendship.

After that, PZ would call me to come over to Jersey for an occasional gig, and we would chat from time to time. Eventually, we started to do the Louis Prima thing as a much smaller act.

In July of 2002, my phone rang and it was PZ. He said, "Eric, are you sitting down?"

I said some low-level obscenity, and he said, "No, really. I'm serious. Sit down."

I thought it was a little weird, but he sounded serious. So I sat.

"Your daughter wants to talk to you. I ran into Bruce P. (a former colleague) at the _____ Club in Maryland." By the wildest of coincidences, I had played there the previous week.

Bruce told PZ that he lived next door to her, and that she had asked him about me.

This requires a little background.

In the fall of 1980, a girl I didn't remember sleeping with told me that I was the father of her newborn baby girl. She went on to say that I was to have nothing to do with them—no visits, no communication, and no money.

In my complete degenerate self-centeredness, I perceived that I had dodged a bullet. My life wouldn't have to change. After all, I didn't even know the girl's last name. And jeez, I couldn't even imagine the circumstances under which I would have slept with her.

Later I put it together. It was an act so inconsequential that I didn't even remember it. It had literally been an afterthought to just another drunken night. I'd had hundreds of such nights. It was a lot like the movie *Groundhog Day*.

Even after she gave me this enormous piece of news, I didn't ask her last name. Perhaps, under the circumstances, I was too stunned and embarrassed.

Even as a drunk, I was aware of how low this was. I was mostly able to keep it out of my mind, although every Father's Day, I went to my own little corner of the ninth circle of hell—the one reserved for betrayers of kin.

As I sobered up, I became more acutely aware of what I can only call my sin. If there is such a thing as sin, this more than qualifies. I knew that, at some point, I was going to have to find her and let her do or say whatever it was she needed to do or say to me. I had no idea how to find her. I knew my daughter's first name, but not her last. Her aunt had brought her to a rehearsal when she was three, and they stayed a half hour. Even as I write this, I cringe at my cowardice.

I called the number I was given.

"This number is no longer in service." I learned later that the area code had changed. Not knowing what else to do, I called PZ and got Bruce's number. I gave Bruce my contact information and did what the Third Step had taught me: I gave it to God and let it go.

Summer became fall became winter became spring became June 15, 1993. Father's Day. I had gone to see my own Dad in the nursing home. My thoughts were on him and our formerly complicated relationship. He had Alzheimer's, and it's hard to hold resentment for someone who's no longer there.

I had some time to kill, so I took a walk into the local woods in search of a certain rock formation of which I'd heard. In my wandering, I came upon a clearing in the woods. It seemed to me a spiritual place. As I came to the center of the clearing, it struck me as cathedral-like.

Lately, I hadn't been doing much more than perfunctory praying. "Good morning, God. Please keep me sober." "Good night, God. Thanks for keeping me sober." Nothing much deeper than that. So I thought this would be a good place to pray, to really reach out to the god of my understanding. My Higher Power.

I did. Things hadn't been going terribly well for me of late— relationships, finances, and so on.

"God, Lord of the universe, Great Spirit. Whatever You are, please help me. I have not been very responsible lately. I need to live up to the responsibilities of an adult. I'm an adult now, and I feel as though I should be living up to more of the things adults are supposed to do. Help me to be responsible. Amen."

It wasn't the prayer of St. Francis, but I meant it.

I went to work for a few hours, and when I got home, there was a message on the answering machine.

"Hi. This is Aimeé. Terri's daughter. I just wanted to say Happy Father's Day because I've never had anyone to say it to before."

It didn't know it was possible for one's heart to leap for joy and sink in fear at the same time. It was what I wanted and truly dreaded. I could finally give this young woman the chance to have at me, but I didn't look forward to it.

Then I thought of my prayer, and I thought, "Cute, God. Really cute."

There was little more to the message than the phone number and, "I understand if you don't want to call me back. You don't have to."

I called. We talked for three hours.

I told her that there was nothing I could ever say in the world that would excuse me for my total abandonment of her. She wanted to know about me, and I told her that I was a recovering alcoholic. I had been sober for thirteen years.

Her response was unbelievable.

"I've been sober for two years. I know that if you had been around when I was a kid, you would have been just another drunk in the mix. This way it's better. I get you when you're okay."

That wasn't the first time I wept that day.

She wasn't certain what to call me. I told her it was her choice. I didn't really have the moral authority to make any demands. She has called me Dad ever since.

During the following week, I made the decision that I would never ask for a blood test. I was going to be whatever my daughter needed me to be, no matter the need. I would be her crying cushion or her punching bag. She needed me to be her dad, and I needed to be that for her. However, when I saw her, any questions about my paternity vanished. The similarities were obvious.

She and her boyfriend came to visit me the following weekend. To my family's credit, and in spite of the fact that I had kept this horrible secret from them through all of those years, they threw a huge party for her, welcoming her into the family. It was the start of a warm, loving relationship.

Later that weekend, a seemingly insignificant thing happened. It is an understatement of epic proportions to say that I am a fan of the soul band Tower of Power. The first time I heard them it changed the course of my life. Until then, I was an aspiring young classical trumpet student. After hearing them, I realized what else could be done with horns. I have been playing soul music for thirty-eight years now.

Later, when I was sobering up, I noticed a liner note on a Tower of Power CD that said, "Special thanks to all the friends of Bill W."

Aha, I thought. If they can be sober and in the business, so can I. Thus, I got back into my music and became a better-than-ever player. My reputation rose, and I achieved a certain amount of career redemption. That was the second time they changed my life.

The insignificant thing was this: I put a Tower of Power CD in my car stereo. Aimeé loved them. She had never heard of them and went fairly wild.

Over the course of the next month, Aimeé and I saw each other weekly and spoke by phone every day. Then I got the Tower of Power monthly email, which included their concert schedule. There were going to play a free concert in a park, in Camden, New Jersey, not far from where Aimeé was living. I called her and suggested that I take a day off work and come over to Jersey. We would have dinner, then go see the band. She thought it was a great idea, and off we went.

Aimeé is not comfortable in crowds and was a little taken aback by the thousands who showed up. So she and the girlfriend who had come with us spent the whole concert sitting on a beach blanket. She enjoyed the music but didn't really want to stand up.

I, on the other hand, couldn't sit down. And as I was bobbing and weaving to the music, I began to chat and lightly flirt with an attractive, interesting woman who was about my own age standing nearby. It happened that we, by chance and in wildly remote parts of the country, had connections with Louis Prima. She was from New Orleans and had worked on Bourbon Street in a place where he had played, and I had shared a stage with his famed and fabled sax man, Sam Butera.

Though I was a little leery of appearing too forward in front of my newfound daughter, I suggested to this woman that she and I have dinner sometime. I left without finding out what she did for a living, but I asked her when I called the next day.

"Please don't freak out," she said. "I'm a Unitarian Universalist minister." I was, to say the least, surprised. However, I was determined to be cool about it. "Okay. What's a Unitarian Universalist?"

Her explanation of liberal religion, specifically Unitarian Universalism, seemed to fit perfectly with AA's rather libertarian view that it doesn't matter what you call your Higher Power, so long as you call on it. I had wanted to join some kind of church but did not want to join under false pretenses. If I couldn't agree with the creed, I didn't want to sit there pretending to believe, nor did I want to go into someone else's house and tell them what to believe. My own spirituality is a mix of Christianity, Buddhism, Hinduism, Ayn Rand, and whatever else I can find to help me through this life. While my general philosophical outlook is more conservative than the average UU, my spiritual point of view is much more libertarian or liberal. I'm an odd bird in UU circles, but it works for me.

In AA, we try not to talk about theology—what you believe is your business. This is, in my most idealized view, what Alcholics Anonymous and Unitarian Universalism have in common.

In any case, I was intrigued that this woman was extremely cool and a minister. I had never dated a minister. But I've always had something of an adventurous streak in me, so I was not dissuaded.

Something strange happened. After a long and committed bachelorhood, I married Rev. M. Jaws remain dropped in several states.

"Him? He got *married*? He married a *what*???"

In my whole dysfunctional life, my relationships were always about my convenience. This time, I had to change everything in my life and move to her. I became happy and content.

It's funny how that works.

We eventually moved to New Orleans. Within a week of arriving there I encountered a sax player. I had randomly played a set with him three years earlier at my first Mardi Gras. It was my first time in the city, and I had just walked into a club and asked to sit in with the band. The sax player had given me his card, but after a couple of years, I figured I'd never see him again and threw it out.

This kind musician now took me under his wing, and through a series of introductions and sit-ins, by the end of September, I got a full-time job playing on Bourbon Street. Other jobs have come to me from that starting point.

Where did I find this sax player? In an AA clubhouse. He was twelve years sober at that time. In the year that followed, I found that I am more at home in New Orleans than any place I've ever been. I got my career back. I know hundreds of people here. I have a new sponsor. AA has never let me be a stranger for very long, no matter where I go. My wife is happy and I am happy.

This may seem a rather rambling tale, but all of these events stem from the single thought that I owed this man an apology.

From this single application of the Ninth Step, every single aspect of my life changed—forever. AA's Promises are found after the Ninth Step in the Big Book for a reason. They say,

> If we are painstaking about this phase of our development, we will be amazed before we are halfway through. We are going to know a new freedom and a new happiness. We will not regret the past nor wish to shut the door on it. We will comprehend the word serenity and we will know peace. No matter how far down the scale we have gone, we will see how our experience can benefit others. That feeling of uselessness and self-pity will disappear. We will lose interest in selfish things and gain interest in our fellows. Self-seeking will slip away. Our whole attitude and outlook upon life will change. Fear of people and of economic insecurity will leave us. We will intuitively know how to handle situations which used to baffle us. We will suddenly realize that God is doing for us what we could not do for ourselves. Are these extravagant promises? We think not. They are being fulfilled among us—sometimes quickly, sometimes slowly. They will always materialize if we work for them.

Not to Injure Others

Tandi

Boy, was I ticked off when my dad got sober. It was as if he traded in one addiction for another. Rather than lose him to the bottle, I lost him to meetings. Rather than his acting like a drunk jerk, he acted holier than thou.

I remember the family meeting at which my father announced that he had found sobriety with the help of Alcoholics Anonymous. I had just started college. Left the house. And for years I would associate my leaving with his freedom from liquor. Or the converse, I would associate his addiction with my presence, as if it were somehow my fault. Irrational, yes, but this is not a rational disease.

And what difference did his sobriety really make to me? As a drunk, he was not mentally present to me. In high school I was an honor student, cheerleader, drama club member, student council representative, and more. And I don't think he was aware of what or how I was doing. Once he got sober, he was so distracted by AA meetings and a new circle of friends that he never stopped to ask how college studies were going, or if I was meeting new friends at school.

Looking back, I can see we were both self-absorbed. But I had an extra layer of anger. And also guilt. Wasn't I supposed to be happy he was finally sober? Isn't this what I had been praying for my whole life?

If I was going to be pissed, I wanted to know what I was pissed about. I snuck a peek at his Big Book. I could gauge where he was in the Twelve Steps.

I kept waiting for Step Nine. I must be on his Step-Eight list of people to make amends with. I mean, I am his daughter, right?

I even went through his office when he wasn't home, looking for a list with my name on it. I never found one.

And I don't remember him ever asking for forgiveness. Ever making amends with me. Ever going through Step Nine with me. Maybe he did, and I was too angry to recognize it. Maybe I dismissed it because I didn't trust his sobriety. I mean, how many broken promises and apologies have I heard in my lifetime? Maybe it was so foreign, I didn't see it for what it was. But I do know it came.

Growing up, I braced myself for the possibility that my father would die from drunk driving, wrapping the car around a tree and not walking away this time. But his death cruelly came ten years after he chose a life of sobriety. He died of cancer unrelated to alcohol or cigarettes or other drugs.

I flew home to say good-bye as soon as I got the call from my mother that his death was close. As the plane landed, I had what I can only describe as a transcendental experience. The colors all around me suddenly amplified in a burst, and I felt overwhelmed by deep contentment and then peaceful calm. I looked at my watch. 4:18 a.m.

My Aunt Ruthie was there to pick me up. "We need to hurry. He's passing."

I shook my head and told her he had already passed, and it was all fine. We reached the hospital close to 5:00 a.m., and my mother was waiting to take me in to say good-bye to what was left of my father. His consciousness left at 4:15 a.m. according to his medical chart.

Back at my parents' house, I went straight to the closet and pulled out his Navy peacoat and put it on. It still smelled like him. I wore it constantly, only taking it off to shower, until the smell dissipated.

I wandered into his home office and sat in his chair, just staring off into space. All that anger I had harbored over the years was

117

numb. I sensed a storm of emotions fighting it out in my limbic brain, but in my conscious brain was radio static.

Then I spotted the stack. In the middle of his desk sat a mound of papers and envelopes of various sizes. On top of the stack was a scrap of furry brown cloth with fringe. I knew I'd seen this before but couldn't place it. Holding it in my hand, I poked my finger through a buttonhole. This was the tail to my childhood Eeyore. I still had Eeyore at home on my nightstand. I never knew what had happened to his tail. I assumed that I had lost it in one of our many adventures.

Under the tail was a note.

"Punki-pie, Know that I miss you and love you and am very proud of you. I will always be with you. Love, Pop"

In the stack of papers was every note or card I had ever sent him. Crayon letters scrawled with misspellings. Drawings of the two of us. Even a simple note, "Thanks for the car. Will call if we're late. Should be back by midnight. Don't worry about me. I'm designated driver. Love, tk." Birthday cards. There was my life in chronological order. He was present, waiting to capture whatever I sent his way. And he is present with me now.

Along with his Navy peacoat, I also took home his Big Book. It sits on my desk next to the gray hymnal. And Eeyore sits on my nightstand, reunited with his tail. These are symbols of Step Nine complete. Amends made.

My response to my father's sobriety, while probably normal, wasn't very mature, accepting, encouraging, or productive to our relationship at the time. But I trust that we were each doing the best we could do at the time. And isn't that a life-affirming and respectful way to live? Trusting that we're each doing the best we can do with what we have at the time.

It can be complicated and uncomfortable when someone else's path doesn't cross our own as we need it to. It can be painful when our own journey disappoints a person who is important to us. Self-differentiation is a sign of spiritual maturity, when we our own spiritual growth and choices, and accept another's as their own—different from each other even as we're interdependent with one another.

In the end, my father's final message was not only responsible, it was response enabling. He gave me time and space and freedom to seek my own healing as he sought his, but he showed me that he was indeed present, witnessing and loving along the way.

Step Ten

Continued to take personal inventory and when we were wrong promptly admitted it.

Oh Dear God—

I was wrong again! I thought once I had made it this far in the program, I wouldn't make mistakes; wouldn't injure another by my thoughts, words, or deeds. Now I see that this is a lifelong practice and that every day and each encounter provides an opportunity for me to take personal inventory.

God, I pray for the courage to promptly admit when I am wrong and not wait for the perfect opportunity when I have all the right words. Help me to keep it simple. "I was wrong. I messed up. I'm sorry. You deserved better from me." Help me not to deflect or diminish my wrong, but to own up to it with honesty and integrity. I ask for courage and humility in my everyday affairs.

Spiritual Inventory

John

Conscience, if suffered to inspect faithfully and speak plainly, will recount irregular desires and defective motives, talents wasted and time misspent. . . . Shall we retire to rest with a burden of unlamented and unforgiven guilt upon our conscience?
—William Ellery Channing, "Daily Prayer"

By the time I reached Step Ten in my Twelve-Step work, I had worked the previous Nine Steps diligently and with a good sponsor. The promises were really coming true for me, and I was beginning to know "a new freedom and a new happiness." I was definitely not the same person I was when I began to actively work on my recovery.

When I reached that point, my sponsor told me that the first nine steps are the essential elements of creating a stable recovery. The steps that follow—Ten, Eleven, and Twelve—are what might be called the maintenance steps. Alcohol, as our literature says, is "cunning, baffling and powerful." It is also very patient. Even after the arduous, soul-wrenching work of the first nine steps, we cannot take our recovery for granted. The last three steps are not done once and finished, but are activities that we need to establish as daily habits in our lives if we are not to be in danger of losing our recovery.

The steps in a Twelve-Step program of recovery are, my sponsor said, in a particular order for a reason. Each step builds on the ones before. Several previous steps are particularly important in order to establish a solid Step Ten practice. They are:

Step Four: Made a searching and fearless moral inventory of ourselves.

Step Five: Admitted to God, to ourselves, and to another human being the exact nature of our wrongs.

Step Six: Were entirely ready to have God remove all these defects of character.

Step Eight: Made a list of all persons we had harmed, and became willing to make amends to them all.

I took some time to review my work on these Steps. As a result, I got a fairly clear idea of the habits of thought and action, the misperceptions and the blind spots that helped create and reinforce my addiction. I know that in my daily working of Step Ten, I need to look out for blaming others for my moods and feelings, my tendency to harbor resentments, and my need to be the center of attention—whether that means stepping on others in conversation, hogging the floor, or exaggerating to make a story entertaining. I felt especially humbled when my sponsor recommended that I share at meetings only when I was called on, even when I had "brilliant" insights to share on the topic.

At a workshop led by Rev. Rob Hardies on the spiritual practices of early-nineteenth-century Unitarians such as Ralph Waldo Emerson and William Ellery Channing, I was introduced to a practice called *examen*, or meditative self-reflection. Channing described this practice in his pamphlet "Daily Prayer." It includes similarities to the Step Ten practice in the Twelve Steps and the Twelve Traditions book, but goes into greater detail.

I use Channing's practice as adapted by Hardies. I do this practice near the end of the day, in bed, before I go to sleep. It doesn't take long. Five minutes is enough. I close my eyes as I relive the events of the day, starting from when I got up to the moment of beginning the examen. I notice what I did and how I felt about it. I find these questions helpful:

- When did my best, wisest, and most loving self show up during the day?

- Was I able to accept the things I could not change with serenity?

- Do I have the courage to work to change what I could change?

- Was I confused about what I could change and what I couldn't?

- Did any of my unhelpful tendencies—in Twelve-Step language, my character defects—show up today?

- Did I take responsibility for my emotions, or did I blame someone else for them?

- Self-pity is deadly for an addict. Did I act out of self-pity today?

- Did I take someone else's inventory, dwelling on their flaws?

- Did my actions harm anyone, even a little bit? Am I willing to admit I was wrong to them?

Sometimes I need to remember not to use this personal inventory to beat myself up. As we say in AA, "We strive for progress, not perfection." This is an opportunity to learn, to protect my recovery, and to grow in happiness and serenity.

The second part of the examen is to make some resolves for the next day. My inventory points the way. It tells me what I must accept and what might be the next right thing to do, if I have the courage. It brings awareness to my positive and less positive tendencies. Then I can resolve to admit I was wrong to anyone I may have hurt and to make amends if necessary. I have to be careful of my tendency to weasel out and not do the amends, making up some kind of excuse.

The final part of this practice is to dwell for a moment on the one thing about the day that I am most grateful for. I try to take this final attitude of gratitude into my sleep with me, letting go of everything else. I leave the day and its concerns with God, knowing I have done my part of the work.

I find it powerful to add two other practices to my day that allow me to take personal inventory. They take very little time and make a big difference in how I live my day. These practices are praying over my schedule and praying over my emails. Before I begin my workday, I look over my schedule and notice how I feel about each appointment or task. Do I feel anxious about this meeting? What is that about? How can I approach this event in my schedule with something other than dread? Can I bring curiosity to the situation? Can I resolve to act differently this time? What is the next right thing I can do to bring a positive resolution to the meeting or event? What do I need to do so that I can feel that I've done all I can and let go of the outcome? Perhaps the next item in my schedule leaves me with a feeling of excitement or anticipation. I feel gratitude for that. As I look at the balance of events in my schedule, I may wonder how to bring three positives to each stressful event or task in the future. How can I plan to bring this about? I pray that I will bring wisdom and love to each situation. I then go on with my day.

Before I open my email, I pray for wisdom and a mind of love and compassion. I've created a fun prayer that I often say to myself: "God grant me the serenity to delete what I can, the courage to actually do something about the things that are my responsibility, and the wisdom to know the difference." I delete vigorously! I look over the emails that are left and say a little prayer for everyone who has communicated with me and ask God's assistance to be helpful and wise in my replies.

Another time to do a quick personal inventory is when I find myself upset. In the Twelve Steps and Twelve Traditions book, there is a statement that is sometimes difficult for addicts to accept: "It is a spiritual axiom that every time we are disturbed no matter what the cause, there is something wrong with us." Along with self-pity, resentments are deadly for an addict. So when I am upset, I stop and do a spot inventory. What have I contributed to this situation? What were my expectations for this person or situation that were not met? I love the AA slogan, "Expectations are pre-planned resentments." Other people do engage in hateful behaviors. So do I. I can practice the same forbearance toward others that I would wish for myself. Again, from the Twelve and Twelve: "It will become more and more evident as we go forward that it is pointless to become angry, or to get hurt by people who, like us, are suffering from the pains of growing up." If we examine our own behavior and attitude, we can prevent words or actions that could damage a relationship and create suffering for hours, days, and years to come.

Before I descended into alcoholism, I had a vital and regular Buddhist meditation practice, which included attending a retreat lasting several days at least once a year. My practice gradually fell away as my drinking got worse. Meditation is all about honesty, and addiction is all about denial. Since my recovery, I have joyfully reclaimed my meditation practice, including attending retreats even more frequently. In my meditation practice I can have both a broader and a deeper view of my strengths and joys, my spiritual progress, and the patterns of self-imposed suffering that may have been only partially conscious.

If in any of these inventories I find that I have been wrong or have harmed somebody, it is vital that I admit it as quickly as possible. The hardest thing is to admit it first to myself. This is because human beings, especially addicts, are great at rationalization. I say things to myself like, "It was really his fault," or "I had a right to tell her that," or "I wasn't gossiping. It's important for people to know what she's really like," or "I wasn't trying to show how much smarter I was than everyone else. I was contributing to the conversation," or "Maybe I exaggerated a little (or a lot), but it made for a better story," or "That may have been a fib I told, but in spirit, it was the truth." These are deeply entrenched habits of thought and speech. Again, we strive for progress, not perfection. Every time we catch ourselves in a rationalization and admit it to ourselves, we begin steadily to uproot these habits.

Before I worked all the other steps leading to Step Nine, I dreaded this process and wondered how I could possibly do it. When I expressed this concern to my sponsor, he replied, "Just take one step at a time. Don't think about that yet." But now I have the experience of having done the Step and I have the relief and serenity that comes from doing all in my power to release the hold of the past. That makes it even more important to not let hurts, slights, and insults fester and grow. If I was wrong, I need to admit it now. I need to concentrate on my part of the hurt, not on theirs. I cannot control their reaction or opinion of me. I can only do my best to repair what I am responsible for.

Often the act of admitting I was wrong is much simpler than I fear. "I apologize for my tone of voice earlier when we were discussing the budget." "If I had it to do over again, I wouldn't have initiated a conversation about your sister when I was tired and hungry. I'll try to remember next time." "I've thought over what you said yesterday, and I now think you were right about a lot of the points you made." "I'm sorry I got so angry with you when we were talking politics last week. I forgot that our relationship is much more important than that you agree with my political opinions." It can be hard to apologize, but the skill of doing so in a timely way is one of the most important of all interpersonal habits to cultivate. I try to remember how I felt when someone admitted to me that they were wrong and sincerely apologized.

The process of engaging with this Step, of taking a spiritual inventory, is not something that a person does once and then is finished with it. The beauty of this Step is that there are daily opportunities to practice it: by realizing one was wrong, by acknowledging damage that may have been done, and, as the Step asks us, to promptly admit it. Because of this Step, I've found a new freedom from fear, guilt, and brokenness, and for that, I'm truly grateful.

Right Relationship

Katie

I remember that when I was a new Unitarian Universalist minister, a local veteran colleague persistently interrogated ministry tenderfoots like me: "How's your prayer practice?" Defensively, I felt, Hey! I was pretty good at being a spiritual person, and it didn't seem that a prayer practice was the be-all and end-all to a strong ministry. I soon discovered that the work of being a professional clergyperson, and for that matter, the job of being fully alive, balanced, and engaged in this world could kick my derriere.

I found that fully undertaking the Twelve Steps as a way of living has become a healthy response to filling a painful void in my life. It was that same hungering I had previously misunderstood and acted upon in destructive ways, that very longing that I sometimes hear referred to as the "God-sized hole." I was critical in my observations, thinking that it was a quality that made me seem wise, rather than a tedious know-it-all. I tended to be insensitive to others but ultra-sensitive to my own needs and impulses. I imagined that in my desperation to have my desires quenched and indulged, I was somehow more savvy and creative than you. As my husband puts it, "I didn't know how to be comfortable when I was uncomfortable."

Step Ten reminds me of the necessity of having a *daily* spiritual practice. This vital practice of taking a personal inventory is often thought of in business vernacular as tallying up the stock on the shelves—removing the dented cans, checking the expiration dates. As religious liberals, we might infuse it with a more sacred tone by referring to it as coming into right relationship.

Rather than looking outward at the world, we are required to look inward, to do not just self-reflection, but some self-correction. It is so much easier to look at the world and others around us and be the wise uber-critic. Alternately, when we are hard on ourselves, we usually unduly pick at the things that can't be changed or engage in self-pity, rather than looking at the things that *can be changed* and doing something about them.

Step Ten is a significant spiritual practice, not to be taken lightly. If I'm going to take my personal inventory, I've got to do so sincerely. This demands honesty, selflessness, and a lack of fear. It's often said in Twelve-Step meetings, and even from Unitarian Universalist pulpits, that the opposite of fear is faith, and our best attempts at faith are needed for taking on this daily exercise.

Our spiritual forefather, Ralph Waldo Emerson, wrote about this vulnerable spiritual entryway into the soul. "Faith and love are apt to be spasmodic in the best minds," he shared. "Men live on the brink of mysteries and harmonies into which they never enter, and with their hand on the door-latch, they die outside." For me, this is a great descriptor of how my life and my spiritual growth have deepened through taking the Twelve Steps and making them a continuing part of my life. They help me to truly enter life and not "die outside."

It can be so easy for us to skirt the edges of a spiritual path when we've got a religious community to hold us up. But our free faith brings with it responsibility too, responsibility to determine our own credo and to deepen our own spiritual path. Step Ten is the gentle nudge I need to make that penetrating effort. Each day, and throughout the day, I need to continuously examine my actions, my motives, my voice. I might start out well-intentioned, but the first time someone doesn't use their turn indicator or disagrees with me in a meeting, I can get thrown off course. I have to pause, *right in the moment*, and get out of my own way.

Sometimes I'll insist on something, only to find out later that I'm wrong, that I've stepped on others' opinions, or that the sound from my mouth is not the tone and pitch that lead to pleasant communication. It's best to correct my behavior right away, to apologize or otherwise make amends. The sooner I take corrective action, the more likely it is to be a smaller job and leave me with a clear head, freed from leftover negativity.

I practice other spiritual disciplines in addition to the Tenth Step. I do centering prayer and I practice yoga with much joy and enthusiasm, but I've discovered that it's not enough to do any of those things if I treat others, or myself, with a lack of respect. The spiritual practice of Step Ten—taking personal inventory on a daily and even hourly basis, and then when I'm wrong, dealing with it rather than letting it pile up—helps me become more spiritually and emotionally balanced.

I have to carefully watch for justifiable anger. Resentments lead to a rotten day. And holding on to them can be more dangerous, leading to the negative addictive behavior of former days. This behavior can be a direct route to a sure death or to an utterly miserable and unhappy life. I've got to identify those resentments when they pop up, analyze what's going on with me, and take action to let them go. I've got to give them over to a Higher Power. As a faithful agnostic, my Higher Power is my faith that, although I may not know for sure if there is a God, in the words of the spiritual, "over my head, I hear music in the air." The most important feature of this Higher Power is that it's not me.

So during the day, I pause to ask myself, "Where am I?" "Where am I going?" I can't put off these questions until the day when things are tough; I have to ask them each day to stay emotionally and spiritually balanced. I know that it's not easy to do this every day. Like most of us, my life is full. The calendar is booked. I've got to keep track of my family, my physical health, my congregation, and my duties therein. But I want to do these things well. So I have helpers.

I wear a purple bracelet as a reminder to watch for complaining and criticizing. I carry in my purse some business-card-sized pamphlets I can pull out when necessary. My favorite is a tattered pink card with the title "Emotional Maturity." The message inside reads, "The mature person has developed attitudes in relation to herself and her environment which have lifted her above 'childishness' in thought and behavior." The message comes from "Moral and Spiritual Values in Education," created in the early 1950s and used in the Los Angeles City Schools. Characteristics of this mature person include being able to accept criticism gratefully, being glad for an opportunity to improve, meeting emergencies with poise, not having feelings easily hurt, and being a good loser. This person lives by the spiritual essence of the Great Commandment, "You shall love your neighbor as yourself."

One of the most crucial helpers in staying in right relationship is talking to another person, like my sponsor. I check in with her regularly. She knows me well—my strengths and flaws. She isn't afraid to look in my mirror alongside me and tell me what she sees. She gives the gift of honest feedback. Does she see me carrying around a resentment I'm blind to, or one to which I grasp tightly? Insisting on keeping these feelings can contribute to a lint-roller of a negative day, picking up bitterness and annoyances like so much pet hair. My sponsor or another close friend can help me laugh at myself and let go of this pain, shedding my shortcomings and acknowledging my blessings.

Each of our liabilities has a contrasting asset. When I feel or act resentful, it is also possible to generate forgiveness. When I'm working on a big pity party, I can strive for self-forgetfulness. When I'm into justification, I can aim for humility. When my foot is tapping and my fingers are rapping against the desk in impatience, I can choose to take a deep breath into patience.

This is what I strive for. It's what I call being spiritually fit or emotionally grounded or maybe even being a bodhisattva. It's certainly the way I want to be. Some days, it comes more naturally than others. On those other days, I have to work hard not to be my two-year-old self. Some days, it's all I can do not to pout, throw tantrums, feel jealous, or be the number-one champion complainer. I need all the tools hanging in my shed to clean up my act.

But these kinds of days come less frequently now, and the spikes on the graph are less pointy. Now I've got little molehills rather than steep mountains to climb. I know my tools well; my helpers have now become my friends. I open the book (the Big Book or any spiritual or meditation manual I've got by my bedside) first thing in the morning, I begin with a healthy breakfast, and I do all I can about getting enough sleep. It isn't so hard to right myself when I tip over.

Long ago, the Apostle Paul counseled to "pray without ceasing." He might have been practicing Step Ten. Nowadays, if I'm asked, "So how's your prayer practice?" I can give an honest, affirmative response. I know how to live a day at a time, and I try my best to practice it, daily.

Step Eleven

Sought through prayer and meditation to improve our conscious contact with God *as we understood Him*, praying only for knowledge of His will for us and the power to carry that out.

Mindfulness with Breath Practice

Begin by taking this one seat, wherever we are. Sitting with an intention to be here. Willing to be present with life as it is, and just as we are right now. This is the moment we have.

Becoming conscious of the breath. Breathing in and breathing out. Basic breathing, noticing if the breath is shallow or deep, fast or slow.

Checking in with the physical sensations of breathing. Noticing the breath as it enters the nostrils. Becoming aware of congestion or ease in breathing. Of moisture or dryness.

Following the breath down into the throat and the upper chest. Noticing the expanding of the rib cage, the lungs filling with air. Checking in with sensations in the belly as the in-breath is completed. Noticing the pause before the exhalation begins.

Breathing out, focusing the attention in the belly and chest, releasing the air. Again, noticing pace, pressure, or any other physical sensations in the body as we're breathing out. Getting in touch with moisture, dryness, whatever is present as the breath leaves the body through the mouth or nostrils.

Then, checking in with the pause, however long or short it is, before the next in-breath. And becoming aware as the cycle of in-breath and out-breath begins once more.

For the next few moments in the silence, inviting the awareness to rest on the waves of breath. Breathing, in and out. Out and in.

(After as many minutes of silence as you'd like)

Knowing in this moment of this simple vow to be with our breath, that as a teacher once said—if we're aware of the fact of our breathing, then we can remember that there is so much more right with us than there is wrong with us.

Will and Power

Sarah

If I Did Not Pray

I could not move against this wind if I did not pray.
And all that is said of me that is untrue
would make lame my gait if I
could not free myself from
the weight of others'
malice.

I could not move against all His light
if I did not pray.

See how things become; what a change
can happen, when we find a way
to keep Him
close.

—Rabia of Basra, translated by Daniel Ladinsky

For the longest time, I thought that God belonged to others. I grew up in a small Unitarian Universalist fellowship in central Minnesota, where I learned the stories, traditions, rituals, and doctrines of other religions. I didn't feel as though I was being asked to reflect on what I, as a Unitarian Universalist, believed. I felt like I was on the outside looking in on other peoples' understandings and experiences of God. However, after embarking on my spiritual journey through the Twelve Steps of Alcoholics Anonymous, I have to come to realize and appreciate the skills for spiritual growth that I learned through Unitarian Universalism.

My drinking career was relatively short-lived. I began in earnest at sixteen, when painful changes swept through my life uninvited. I found myself without tools and without the skills to cope, to see beyond my circumstances, or to gain any kind of perspective about my life. My reason and intellect failed me, and I resorted to justified anger. I stewed in the perceived injustice of my life and fell into a self-centered, self-pitying abyss of darkness. I found myself as a suicidal alcoholic, quietly drinking my anger, fears, and insecurities away. By nineteen, I had learned to meet my daily obligations so I could get drunk and drift off into a peaceful sleep. Sleeping and drinking were each day's goals. Everything in between was simply a means to an end, a means to justify my behavior and keep the parents off my back.

Just before my twenty-first birthday, I was introduced to a sober alcoholic. He and his friends quietly and patiently brought me into their circle, and through fellowship, I was introduced to the program of Alcoholics Anonymous. On March 1, 1997, at the age of twenty-one, I embarked on my journey of sobriety, and today I have enjoyed twelve years of clean and sober living. In sobriety, I have found the meaning of joy and gratitude, the power of perspective, and the value of having a personal relationship with a Higher Power I call God.

At about the same time my drinking began, I also developed an interest in spirituality. While I drank out loud, screaming to be punished, I also began to hide my spiritual reading under my bed. When I was certain no one was looking, I would pull it out, looking for solace, guidance, and the wisdom I was convinced my parents lacked. Not until I was introduced to that group of sober drunks did I find permission to pull my spiritual interests out from under my bed and to pursue spirituality in the light of day.

Ten months from the time I was introduced to AA, I finally understood how alcohol contributed to my own misery, and I began attending meetings for myself. As a good UU, I questioned the Twelve Steps at first. I wasn't willing to admit my powerlessness or my insanity. I certainly questioned the wisdom of taking advice from the self-professed "insane." No, I remained skeptical, and to some extent I still do. But it was through Step Eleven that I found a doorway into the program and recovery, and an invitation to develop a relationship with something greater than myself.

Step Eleven, for me, was immediately doable. There wasn't much I could do or admit to in the beginning. But I could learn to pray. To some extent, I had always wanted to learn to pray. The suggestions and guidelines laid out in the Big Book asked me to be open-minded, to commit to a daily practice, and to use prayer and meditation to look outside myself for a larger perspective. I found much freedom in this Step. The search for truth and meaning suddenly came with a how-to guide. Step Eleven offered me a real opportunity to develop my own theology and practice free from expectations, dogma, or rules. It encouraged me to look to the world's religions to inspire my spiritual life, to use what proved to be meaningful, what challenged me and asked me to grow—and to leave behind what held me back and failed to shine a light on the road ahead.

In the beginning, prayer was a foreign language with a weird ritual. Meditation felt silly. In fact, they both did. The daughter of English professors, I relied on the two things I was comfortable with, reading and writing. And so I began a daily practice of reading meditations, journaling, writing letters to God, and keeping gratitude lists. You won't find me kneeling at my bedside; rather, I tend to be buried in a pile of books, pen and journal in hand, a steaming cup of coffee within arm's reach. I make an effort to practice every day. There are plenty of times when my list of excuses is long, and I fail. But with each new day comes a new opportunity to recommit.

I am deeply rewarded every time I commit to making that connection with my higher power. It is the most authentic act and moment of my day. In these daily moments of meeting with God, I know myself to be most loved and accepted, seen and heard. Peace fills my heart, gratitude overwhelms me, joy bubbles up, and I am ready to greet each day. There is no lack—I am whole already—and each event, opportunity, person, or conversation is a gift for me to learn more about myself, life, and God. Each misstep is a chance to practice forgiveness, to know myself more fully and to step closer to the God of my understanding.

My early reading included Marianne Williamson and Neale Donald Walsh—their new-age ideas introduced to me a Higher Power that I could relate to, not one entrenched in the ritual, language, and traditions of others. They spoke of understanding and relating to God in new ways. They seemed to relate experiences of God in present time—the transcending mystery and wonder some call God was alive and well, accessible to all and not left behind in biblical times. More recently, I've come to read more traditional and religious writings, and have developed an affinity for the mystics of the world's religions. Through them I find the experience I know to be true, written about in the language, the history, the mores, and expectations of their time. I've learned to appreciate one's love for God and that longing I believe we all have to know God, to know our source, to know love, and to know ourselves.

Step Eleven brought spirituality out of the musings of my intellect and into the experience of my heart and soul; it came to life. Spirituality has become a habit, a practical experience, not a philosophical idea. I am no longer interested in being right or wrong. Rather, I seek to be connected to spirit, to live with peace, serenity, and an overflowing fountain of joy. In my daily practice, I grow and cultivate gratitude, acceptance, and love. This is what religion and faith are about for me, and why they are important. I had long ago learned there was room for all the world's religions, and now I understand why.

Twelve years in, I have come to rediscover the lessons of my faith. As a UU, I don't so much follow a path to God, but rather build one. I am grateful to have been raised in a faith that believes in me enough to grant me the freedom to blaze my own trail. I am just as grateful that the program of Alcoholics Anonymous and the Eleventh Step have given me the tools to keep me focused, and when necessary, to find my way back when I get lost in my wild meanderings.

Conscious Contact

Ken

I do know how to pay attention . . . how to be idle and blessed . . .
  —Mary Oliver

If I had to pick one image to represent my inner life when I was an active alcoholic, it would be a cartoon character whose upper half stands upright while its legs whirl wildly below. The animated character makes no movement forward. The legs just keep spinning until the character falls over, exhausted.

Expending energy without making progress—that's what my drinking life was like. It was an experience of being divided against myself, distracted by feelings of inadequacy, resentment, and despair. With this torrent of thought and emotion going on inside me, I most often felt alienated from others. I felt like I was racing but not getting anywhere. Fortunately, after a few half-hearted attempts to quit drinking, I finally became overwhelmingly tired because of all the energy I was wasting. Blessedly, I was spent.

One of the initial pieces of inherited wisdom I heard when I got sober was that it takes the first five years of our sobriety just to locate our marbles, and the second five years to learn how to play with them. In my experience, this has been absolutely true.

The first five years after I quit drinking was kind of like discovering that a valuable suitcase with critically important contents that I'd strapped to the hood of my car had been dislodged mid-journey. If I ever hoped to reach my destination, I had no choice—I had to go back and pick up the items scattered alongside miles of road. I made amends to people I hurt. I accessed long-buried feelings of fear and resentment and shame. I began to understand the habits and defects that fed my alcoholism.

This personal archaeology healed many of those rifts, and I'm certain that this healing work will continue as long as I'm alive. What I found wasn't all wreckage, however; there was also buried treasure. These innate and beneficial qualities—a hunger to connect, to love, and to be of use to others and myself—had been there all along.

My years of drinking hadn't obliterated their presence within me, but my active alcoholism had made these qualities feel inaccessible. Frustrated by my seeming inability to maintain consistent contact with a more healthy and holy way of living, and scared that I was innately inadequate to the task of living a committed, accountable, and fully present life, I took refuge in alcohol—which of course made me less committed, accountable, and present, so I took more refuge in alcohol. And there is the awful inner logic and downward spiral of addiction.

When I was drinking, I yearned and reached for spiritually rich connections via wholly inadequate means, like a surgeon attempting a heart operation using rusty tweezers. The truth is, I used to love the intensity of the high. It offered me a sense of transcendence, the feeling of being unbounded by my usual fears and limitations. But that was unconscious contact with my life, unmindful experience, sometimes accompanied by harsh words or unkind actions toward myself or others. Most of the time no obvious damage occurred when I drank, but the feeling of release was temporary, the sense of connection illusory.

I sought escape in my drinking—cheap, transitory transcendence. My artificial high was invariably followed by an artificial low, a depressed state of woe-is-me melancholy and fear, like a pump-and-dump stock, superficially inflated and then punishingly corrected via guilt, shame, and regret.

When I got sober at the age of thirty-five, I started to discover that I had been an extremely poor steward of my life's basic energy, and more specifically, my core spiritual aspirations. As I maintained continuous sobriety over days, then weeks, then years, I started to recognize the core of wholeness that still existed within me, that I had inherent worth and dignity, and that waking up to a different, nondrinking way of life was an expression of that innate capacity for basic goodness. I also knew that my inherent worth and dignity wasn't a static quality, something that would just be developed and matured by accident. I had lived a long time with the chronic dis-ease that came from worry, anxiety, and estrangement. Reforming my habits of heart and mind required a diligence that was foreign to me as a drinker. I needed, as the Eleventh Step describes, a spiritual practice, a means of shaping and remaining accountable to my spiritual aspirations.

I had an immature hide-and-seek attraction to contemplative practices over the years. I would engage with meditation or contemplative prayer here and there but wouldn't allow myself to build up anything like a regular practice. My fundamentally undisciplined life of course had no room for the discipline of a spiritual practice.

A few years after getting sober, I was in a colleague's library one day and came across an old bound copy of William Ellery Channing's nineteenth-century sermon "Likeness to God." These old words landed simultaneously in mind, heart, and gut:

> [Our likeness to God] has its foundation in the original and essential capacities of the mind. In proportion as these are unfolded by right and vigorous exertion, it is extended and brightened. In proportion as these lie dormant, it is obscured.

In my life I'd known considerable, often exhausting, expenditures of energy, but "right and vigorous exertion"? Not so much. Channing's words echoed what I'd read from Tara Brach, John Kabat-Zinn, and Thich Nhat Hanh, who all emphasized the practice of mindfulness, learning to regularly open our awareness and pay attention, moment by moment, to what was happening in our lives.

And instead of just reading about mindfulness, I knew I had to practice to allow the "original and essential capacities of the mind" to brighten and flourish. I didn't half-ass it on my own this time, as I had many times before. I paid for classes in mindfulness training. I showed up week after week. I surrendered to the teaching and practice. I allowed myself to be a beginner, something that terrified me when I was drinking. I missed so many opportunities over the years to grow because I was scared of admitting the words that I now find liberating: I don't know.

I now find that the ongoing blessings of my recovery are most realized through the power of daily mindfulness meditation. It is the power of shaping, sharpening, and deepening awareness that most calls to me as I move more deeply into my sobriety. The wisdom of the scriptures, "Be still, and know that I am God," is revealed to me. I don't apprehend this knowing like picking up information in a book. It is more a process of cultivation than comprehension—the way a gardener strives diligently to create the right conditions for the seed to grow but is personally unable to command that the seed must grow.

I can't exactly describe how that growth is going on within me. However, I do directly experience the fruits of my sitting. Less aimless worry, more honest action. Less despair, more resilience. Less fear, more love. Moving away from the depressing inner logic of an active alcoholic, I encounter an affirming logic in this way of living. The more I sit, the more I experience conscious contact with the God of my understanding and with my life, and that feeds my ongoing aspiration to maintain my practice.

With a sober friend, I've started a group called Mindful Recovery. This weekly, ninety-minute meeting integrates the Twelve Steps with contemplative practice. It is open to anyone following any recovery path and begins with twenty minutes of seated meditation. After that, the meeting opens to a discussion that may be about the Four Noble Truths or about aspirations that help us grow along the path of recovery—gratitude, open-mindedness, humility.

I continue to attend more traditional Twelve-Step meetings, but Mindful Recovery is the group I treasure most, and not because it's "mine." (In fact, it's been a gift for me to start it and then hand over its leadership to others.) I love the richness of our silent sitting together, the explicit and implicit knowledge that, whatever our addiction was or is, we're all aspiring to wake up from unhealthy ways of living to more loving, kind, and attentive ways of being alive. When we do speak of our struggles and victories in recovery, we express a welcome diversity of spiritual perspectives, all grounded in the unity of our common aspirations to wake up.

I hear the echoes of Thoreau's encouragement:

We must learn to reawaken and keep ourselves awake, not by mechanical aids, but by an infinite expectation of the dawn, which does not forsake us in our soundest sleep. I know of no more encouraging fact than our unquestionable ability to elevate our lives by a conscious endeavor. It is something to be able to paint a particular picture, or to carve a statue, and so to make a few objects beautiful; but it is far more glorious to carve and paint the very atmosphere and medium through which we look.

Shaping the means and medium through which I am aware allows me to have more conscious contact with my life. When I sit in meditation on a daily basis with no agenda other than to be present to my life, I find I am better equipped to share a more grounded presence with others, to be curious about their experience, and to be more compassionate and kind toward them and toward myself. I am better able to perceive, as the Quakers say, that which is of God in us, and to let it be.

My experience and understanding of God's will is the easing of my ego. Imperfectly—and often with a struggle that I at least now perceive accurately as struggle, rather than valiance—I'm learning to stop clinging to my story, my way, my version of events as I believe they must be. Much like the breath that anchors my meditation, I find I can take life in, and let life go, with greater ease and well-being than I once knew. When I do, I find that I love better and more wisely, and that I am of more use in this life. All along, this was what I wanted. Now I finally know how to do it.

Step Twelve

Having had a spiritual awakening as the result
of these steps, we tried to carry this message to
alcoholics, and to practice these principles
in all our affairs.

O Thou Love, that has carried me through the darkest
times,
I am full of gratitude for the wisdom I have received
from this program.
The stories of struggle have touched me,
The practice of these Steps has changed me,
The goodness of sobriety has held me all the days of my
life,
And I have found contentment at last.

And yet—it is not my contentment alone,
For I now live not for myself, but for others
For those who are living in fear and self-loathing,
For those whose families have been damaged by
addiction,

For all the pain which cannot be fully repaired,
I dedicate my life to the service of others.

May the result of this practice be a life transformed;
Mine—and others who may benefit from my
*   experience;*
May this spiritual awakening continue on,
Until the dayspring breaks—and the shadows of
*   addiction, flee away.*
Amen.

The Practice of Principles

Jim

My name is Jim. I'm sixty-two and an active member of my Unitarian Universalist congregation. I am also an alcoholic and have been in recovery for the past twenty years. By the grace of God, an ever-loving family, and the fellowship of Alcoholic Anonymous, I have discovered a new way of living, one that faces life issues with humility, clarity, and integrity. I have discovered a life that involves connecting with people, giving freely of myself, and learning how to open up and share with others my gifts as well as my challenges. After many years of working the Twelve Steps of AA and practicing its principles in all my affairs, I have been afforded many new opportunities for growth and have experienced a spiritual awakening. For me, my involvement in the fellowship of AA and my Unitarian Universalist congregation run parallel to my development as a responsible, caring, accountable member of society. Both groups have renewed my faith, hope, and spirituality. They are intertwined and will continue to charge my soul as I follow this lifelong journey.

Three events have impacted my life and been catalysts for my transition from a self-centered, selfish, immature "taker" to the person I am today, one who is grounded in honesty and compassion for others.

I was raised in a very devout Catholic family of four. Although my parents were good, loving providers, very little affection was shown in the household. In retrospect, I experienced low self-esteem and had little self-confidence when relating to others at social events. In my formative years, I never felt that I fit in. At seventeen, I began using alcohol to help quell my anxieties and bolster my sense of self-worth, temporarily masking my insecurity. My parents were not heavy drinkers, but it was obviously in my DNA. My mother's only brother died of alcoholism, and my grandfather abandoned his young family and died in the gutter in New York City. I don't blame my alcoholic behavior on my family, but it is an important piece of the puzzle.

Some way, somehow I managed to graduate from the University of Delaware, get married, and enter the US Army, all in 1969. My dependence on alcohol to get through life during this period was becoming more apparent to my parents. Yet despite their awareness of the problem, they continued to deny it, perhaps because it was just too painful for them to deal with yet another member of the family afflicted by addiction. I realize that I caused them a great deal of heartache and anxiety, and for that I will always be truly sorry. They were not aware, however, of the extent of the damage I was doing to my marriage. It—and I— were in deep, deep trouble.

Fast forward to 1992. By that time, I was raising three children. Two were graduating from high school and college. I myself had just graduated from getting drunk at neighborhood parties and work-related events to now drinking in secret every day. I began to feel isolated, riddled with shame and despair. This secretive pattern of drinking had become necessary because I had promised my wife, Cindy, that I had quit for good in 1990. The secretive drinking was precipitated by me losing my job. I hid bottles of vodka all through the house—the garage, the basement, my golf bags. Although I was able to function on most days, my life had become unmanageable. Furthermore, my marriage was on the rocks, and I was now physically and emotionally addicted. These two years would be the most painful of my life because I was living a lie every day. That is, until June 10, 1992.

On that day, my middle daughter was graduating from high school. I drank about a half pint of vodka straight before we left for the ceremony. Needless to say, a joyous event turned disastrous, and I made a complete fool of myself as I detoured through a stream of water in my pinstripe suit while walking back to the parking lot. My daughter and wife were furious with me, and I knew I had lost the respect of my family. My life as I knew it was over. So when I got home, I proceeded to drink until I passed out. Same story the next day.

On Friday, June 12, my daughter was to move into the dorm at Millersville University for summer session. I had a horrific hangover, and she was, unfortunately, relying on me to help her move. After trying to do so for about half an hour, I was physically unable to continue. Feeling so sick that I had to sit on the curb for the rest of the morning, I experienced overwhelming shame and guilt. As my wife drove me home, my face began to go numb, and my hands started shaking. This was my breaking point, my bottom. I started to sob uncontrollably and cried out to God to help me stop drinking. As I reflect back on it now, I believe this was my spiritual awakening. I was reaching out for some Higher Power to come into my life and give me the courage to stop drinking, because I was unable to do it on my own.

My wife, although deeply concerned, honestly was no longer sympathetic to this pathetic situation and announced that she was calling for an intervention with the family on Saturday. As I would learn later, my detox started on that trip home and continued all through Saturday. During the intervention, Cindy laid out explicitly to my parents the exact nature and depth of my addiction. Since I had already surrendered the fight of trying to control my drinking on my own, I agreed to call a friend and find an AA meeting on Sunday. The intervention was devastating to my parents. My mother was distraught, and I will always remember my father saying, "Jim, you are such a mess. I'm so disappointed and saddened. What are we going to do with you?" These words deeply affected me, and I would reflect on them as my recovery started.

I immediately felt at home when I attended my first meeting that eventful Sunday night. I was in awe of the compassion and respect these strangers bestowed on me. They put me at ease and offered me hope that I could succeed at getting sober. I will always remember their acts of kindness. I truly was beginning a new path to living.

My first AA home group included a diverse cross-section of society. I was so impressed by the outreach of the members, just one alcoholic helping another alcoholic to get sober by serving, caring, and just being there for each other. Just showing up at meetings every day is 80 percent of the solution. Eventually, you regain clarity of thought, your spirituality begins to grow, and your emotional maturation process begins again.

My mother died suddenly on July 30, forty-five days into my sobriety. I was overcome by sadness and regret, especially since I was unable to truly make amends to her. Because my mother was his world, my dad was very distraught over her death, and I felt partly responsible for that. I know in my heart that my addiction put a strain on their marriage and caused a great deal of pain. As I sat silently, comforting my dad at this time of sorrow, I pledged to support him in the coming years. Although my mother was aware of my recovery before she died, she was not able to witness my transformation over these past years. Many years later, reflecting on this still brings tears to my eyes. The day she died was both life ending and life changing. I renewed my commitment to regain my dad's respect. I owed at least this to him and my mother.

My dad lived for many years thereafter, experiencing the positive changes taking place in my life. He was also able to witness my transition from a little boy in an adult body to a responsible, caring adult with an intact family. My association with AA and later with my Unitarian Universalist church helped prepare me emotionally for living life on life's terms.

In recent years I have been afforded the opportunity to apply the Twelfth Step. Twice a week, I drove to Wilmington, Delaware, to tend to my dad's needs. It was both rewarding and fulfilling, and I never regretted the time spent caring for him. Since he was now unable to drive—he had driven until age ninety-four—I became his chauffeur. He appreciated my efforts, which I found comforting. Listening intently to his life stories was an enlightening experience. I spent hours with him talking about family and sports, and I always made a point to express my love for him. As the year went by, he found it easier to express his love. As I was leaving one day, he said, "Jim, I don't know how I would have made it without you." That statement will always remain with me, as I felt redeemed in his eyes. My dad died December 4, 2008, after ninety-five years on this earth.

I have been mentally, emotionally, and physically healthy for a long time. Over the past seventeen years, I've been both diligent and passionate about following the Twelve Steps of AA and have been practicing the principles, especially those described in Step Twelve. I believe that AA is responsible for saving my life. So in return, I feel obligated to extend my hand to newcomers and offer them hope and support so that they may also recover from this addiction. I allocate time each week to attend at least three AA meetings. This practice affords me not only the opportunity to solidify my sobriety, but also to connect with new members who may need direction in how to stop drinking.

It has also been my pleasure to help provide transportation to meetings. A few years ago I took a friend's husband to a meeting every Wednesday for six months. This was my way of paying it forward, with the hope that he would return that favor to someone else in the future. You learn to rely on one another for support. Recently, I've had the occasion to discuss with a member's family the exact nature of the problem and my experience with AA. They were comforted to see direct results of the program firsthand and were reassured that great progress would occur over time.

My relationship with my family, friends, and business associates has improved dramatically, because trust has been restored. That has happened because of my commitment to make amends and a renewed effort to be involved in their daily lives. I do not live in the shadow of their lives anymore and have regained their respect, along with the dignity I had squandered.

Spiritually, I am still developing. Although I had grown in AA by following the Steps and Traditions, I still yearned for a connection with a spiritual community of another nature, one that would truly enhance and motivate spiritual growth. I realized a few years ago that there was still a hole that needed to be filled, and I was only halfway home. This is when I joined a Unitarian Universalist congregation.

I've learned that to benefit fully from the grace I've received, it is imperative that I remain in service, accept my gifts, and share them freely with both groups. I am truly blessed as I continue this journey with renewed purpose and meaning in my life.

A Spiritual Awakening

George

The statement in the Twelfth Step, "having had a spiritual awakening as the result of these steps," is not quite true. Those early AAs had not taken the steps, at least in the format and language prescribed, as the steps had not yet been written. When writing *Alcoholics Anonymous*, AA's founder, Bill W. tried, with suggestions and editing from other members, to bring together the basic ideas this tiny band of newly sober drunks had been working with. They intended to make the Steps subject to individual interpretation—and reinterpretation—as alcoholics try to find spiritual principles that will help them maintain sobriety and live meaningful lives.

In 1949, ten years after the book was published, Bill W. addressed the American Psychiatric Association, stating, "The newcomer merely immerses himself in our Society and tries the program as best he can. Left alone, he will surely report the gradual onset of a transforming experience, call it what he may." In my experience we have a series of awakenings, epiphanies, transforming experiences, or whatever we choose to call them, during our journey in AA. An initial awakening may occur at our first meeting, or perhaps much later. In my case, reading the book before I attended my first meeting irretrievably altered my understanding of my alcoholism, of what lay ahead if I did not change, and of my belief that change was possible. Further awakenings continue to this day.

All AA service has but one purpose: to carry the message of recovery. I have served at various levels of service in AA, but I believe that carrying the message has to begin with helping the newcomer. When talking to a newcomer, I try to welcome them to share in the experience of recovery—to join the club—as an equal, a peer, regardless of how long they have been sober. It is vital for me to both believe and convey that, although I had my last drink over half a century ago, and I have a lot of experience, I do not possess superior wisdom about how to achieve a spiritual way of life that will keep me away from the first drink. I try to share my "experience, strength, and hope" while being clear that I am still looking for solutions, just as they are. An oft-quoted sentence in *Alcoholics Anonymous* refers to "meeting on the road of happy destiny." I try to be clear about something I truly believe: Although I have been walking on the road longer than most, I am in no sense ahead of the newest member—we are walking side by side.

The first message I try to convey to the newcomer is hope—the sense that their life can change, and they can change. Having been around so long, my life, more than my words, has to offer some message of hope. At the same time, I know that a member with just thirty days can seem more amazing and offer more hope to the new person than an old-timer with thirty years.

Once they experience hope, I try to help a newcomer, particularly a sponsee, understand the need to surrender. The surrender begins with accepting that there is no way we can control our drinking. From that point, we need to surrender the belief that we can manage our own lives or the lives of others, and that trying to do so actually makes life unmanageable. We accept that we are not God and cannot be truly self-directed—that we cannot go it alone without help from outside ourselves, whatever we want to call the source of that help. Over the years, I have known atheists and agnostics, as well as those holding conventional religious beliefs, all of whom have found their own way to surrender.

For five decades, I have been given the privilege of sponsoring recovering alcoholics. The simplest definition of a sponsor is someone who will help a newcomer achieve and maintain sobriety. There are no definitive instructions about how to do that, and there are different, often contradictory, approaches. Some AAs feel that you cannot be a friend and a sponsor. I believe that, unless I can primarily offer friendship, I am acting as teacher or counselor, without qualification for either role. So I simply try to be available, to listen with all the patience I can muster, and to avoid telling them what they should do or what they should believe. When I talk about what worked or did not work for me, I do not expect that they will arrive at the same understanding of AA principles. I don't try to impose my understanding of the Steps, but to help them find what works for them, based on their own experience and beliefs—to tell them what I did, not what they should do. I share my belief that the simple suggestions found in the Steps constitute a basis for a spiritual program, not a religious or academic program. They can be learned but not taught. I do not possess expertise about how to use the Steps in one's life and do not believe anyone does, but I am willing to talk for hours to help sponsees find answers that will work for them.

For sponsees who are not theistic, I try to avoid using language about God that sounds very traditional. Atheists and doubters may find the "God stuff" in AA literature unconvincing. I try to emphasize the difference between religion and spirituality, and that the spiritual life that AA helps us to achieve can be different for each of us.

I have no idea how many Fifth Steps I have heard—in which the sponsee admits the exact nature of their wrongs. There have been a lot. I do not have a set of instructions or a formula for this process—each person is different and in a different place in their effort to stay sober. Perhaps the best someone newly sober can do is to admit to some of the wreckage caused by their drinking behavior. At the least, this helps relieve some guilt. Others are ready to talk in depth about all the character defects that have caused themselves and others so much unhappiness. As a sponsor, I try to ask questions, make an occasional pointed comment, and remind them that AA's founder, rather than labeling them as sins, referred to our character defects as "naturally occurring instincts carried to excess." As my sponsor did with me, I try to share enough of my own past and present shortcomings so the sponsee does not feel terminally unique.

As with other relationships, sponsorships do not always work out. I have never asked someone if I could sponsor them; it is up to them to decide whether they want me. My first question to a prospective sponsee is, "What do you expect from a sponsor?" It may not be something I can provide, in which case I suggest they look for someone else. Then there are instances when, after a period of time, the relationship just isn't working. I have rarely given up on anyone, but the sponsee may need something I can't offer and should then try someone else. Other sponsee relationships have lasted for decades and are as close and meaningful as those of family.

The benefits I have received as a sponsor have been immeasurable. Working with newcomers and sponsees has given me the chance to relive my own experience of recovery, and to witness the changes sponsees experience as they find hope, confidence, and joy in sobriety.

Sponsorship provides an opportunity to refresh and rethink my own approach to spirituality. I believe spiritual principles have to be organic rather than static, and that my application of them needs to continue to evolve. As sponsees talk about their problems and the "defects of character" they are dealing with, I realize I not only have had similar problems and shortcomings, but still have some of them, and we can share as equals about how to deal with them. I am provided the opportunity to refresh and rethink my own effort. With long-term sponsees, the relationship is close to co-sponsorship. It can be disconcerting to hear a sponsee refer to long-forgotten advice that you gave them with the suggestion that you might use it yourself.

Now that I am in my eighties, I am increasingly aware of the gift of sponsoring. As we age, the circle of people with whom we are truly connected is likely to shrink. We lose loved ones and people with whom we share a long history. Thanks to sponsorship and AA friendships, I continue to find new people with whom to make a strong and intimate connection. While we do not have decades of shared life experiences, we share a common history of recovery from alcoholism and an ongoing spiritual journey. They seem to want me around—not for the past, but for the present.

The AA old-timers I know and admire have done their best to "practice these principles" in all their affairs, the final thought in the Twelve Steps—as have I. We do not "take" or "work" this part of the Step. It is the foundation for our lives, the ground we stand on, where we seek our identity. For me, it comes down to trying to live a life of love and service, in AA and in my personal and business life, to the best of my often limited ability, based on the spiritual principles found in AA. None of us is completely selfless. I do not always do it well, but I believe the effort to live a life of love and service is the only thing I need to do.

Sometimes the "road of happy destiny" may be a little bumpy or stormy, but we have a great time along the way. On his death-bed, the last words of my sponsor of forty-five years were, "It's been a lot of fun." A few weeks ago, I had a long visit with an AA friend of forty-nine years. We live on opposite coasts now and do not get together often, so our talk lasted for hours. We have both been continuously active in various aspects of AA service. We have experienced both successes and failures in our personal and business lives. We talked about AA friends from the days when we were young and newly sober, and all the crazy things we did. Many of the friends are gone now, and others are scattered from Canada to Belize—we still see or are in contact with a number of them. We talked about our own successes and failures, the mistakes we have made, the things we have done while drinking and in sobriety that we are simply not proud of. And we talked about all the things that have given us a satisfying and happy life. As we parted, my friend said, "And it has *all* been wonderful." I do not quite have my friend's gentle, sunny disposition, yet seriously moved, I had to admit—yes, indeed it has.

Benediction

And you may ask yourself, "My God, how did I get here?"
   —The Talking Heads, "Once in a Lifetime"

The stories in this collection of essays represent a diverse group of Unitarian Universalists: in gender, age, race, class, affectional and sexual orientation, and years of sobriety. Yet all have, at one point, asked the same question: "My God, how did I get here?" *Here* being a place where life has ceased to make sense because of addiction. The authors have taken us to the lowest point in their lives, when it seemed as if there were no good options available.

Fortunately, the stories didn't end there; they began again when the authors decided to enter into recovery. The good news promised by working each of these Twelve Steps is that it works. People have transformed their lives by practicing these Steps, and in the process, they have regained the respect of their spouses, partners, and children, and of their friends and of themselves. At some point, the recovering alcoholic/addict realizes that by practicing these principles in all our affairs, we know exactly "how we got here." We got here—sobriety—by hard work and diligent spiritual practice.

However, we didn't do it alone. We did it by meeting with others in recovery and telling our stories, knowing that they are all utterly unique and profoundly similar. They are the story of the human struggle to feel a part of something greater than oneself, to feel at home in the world no matter where we are. Although most AA meetings end with the Lord's Prayer, a more fitting way to close out a meeting for Unitarian Universalists might be with the benediction by Wayne Arnason:

Take courage, friends.
The way is often hard, the path is never clear
And the stakes are very high.
Take courage, for deep down there is another truth—
You are not alone.

Acknowledgments

For the persistent and faithful editors of Skinner House Books, Marshall Hawkins and Mary Benard; co-author Ken for his original vision of this book; my sponsor, Cathie, whose spiritual guidance has been invaluable to my sobriety; and to the fine people of my Saturday morning Good Stuff home group. Your strength gives me strength and keeps me coming back.
—Cathlean

As noted above, for the support and guidance of Marshall and Mary at Skinner House; co-author Cathlean for her ability to breathe new life into this book when it was very much needed; for Tommy S., my sponsor; and for that old-timer at my first Beginners' Meeting in Flourtown, who said, "We take everyone from Yale to jail here" and I knew that I was welcome. Thank you all.
—Ken

All royalties from the sale of this book will be donated to the Unitarian Universalist Addictions Ministry Team of the Unitarian Universalist Association.

Twelve-Step Terminology

Anniversary/Birthday: The annual marking of the day on which a person got clean or sober, often commemorated with a special coin or chip at a meeting. This is celebrated for people who have continuous recovery from that day.

The Big Book: The book *Alcoholics Anonymous*, containing the foundations of AA teachings as well as the stories of people in recovery from alcoholism. There are now four editions of this book, each one adding personal stories. Other Twelve-Step programs such as Narcotics Anonymous, Overeaters Anonymous, and Adult Children of Alcoholics have their own versions of the Big Book.

Bill W. and Dr. Bob: William Wilson and Dr. Robert Smith, the co-founders of Alcoholics Anonymous.

Experience, strength, and hope: First articulated in the AA preamble, these attributes are shared between people in recovery as they gather to solve their common problem and help others recover.

Friend of Bill/Friend of Bill W.: A way that people in AA or other recovery programs may refer to each other outside of gatherings of the program. If someone hears a person use language that sounds like that used in recovery programs, they might pull that person aside and ask, "Are you a friend of Bill W.?"

Going out: A person who resumes their addictive or compulsive behaviors after a time of sobriety or abstinence. A relapse. Someone may go out for a day or for years. If that person then returns to the rooms, they will often reflect on what it was like for them when they went out, the difficulties they encountered, and what they have learned that they now wish to apply in their recovery.

It works if you work it: Said at the close of meetings to encourage people to keep coming back to the rooms and actively engage in their recovery.

Pink Cloud: A positive feeling of release or liberation from addiction that is common among people in early recovery. This mindset is often viewed with caution, as it may serve as an excuse to avoid the harder work of recovery, such as taking a fearless moral inventory, or it can function as a subtle form of addiction to feeling this way all the time.

The Program: Shorthand for being in recovery, working the Steps, and going to meetings.

The Promises: A description in the book *Alcoholics Anonymous* of the emotional, psychological, relational, and spiritual benefits that can come to a person who diligently works the Steps and remains committed to doing so.

The Rooms: Any location where Twelve-Step meetings occur. These may be a clubhouse that a recovery group may own or rent exclusively for its own purposes, or a rented space in another institution, such as a church basement.

The Serenity Prayer: The most popular and well-known prayer associated with recovery. It is often attributed to theologian Reinhold Niebuhr, although its authorship has never been definitively settled. It is often said at the close of meetings, though sometimes The Lord's Prayer is said instead.

"She/he/they had what I wanted": An expression about what draws someone in recovery to want to work with someone else in recovery, often as their sponsor. It could be a quality of serenity, spiritual maturity, or overall dedication to living a fulfilling sober life.

Sponsor/Sponsee: The voluntary, mentoring relationship between someone in the program with more time and experience in recovery and someone in the program who has less. This is an informal, nonprofessional, but very important part of the Twelve Steps. Newcomers are regularly encouraged to find a sponsor, and this relationship may continue for many years. A sponsee will often choose their sponsor as the person to listen to their Fifth-Step admission. A sponsor also helps to guide a sponsee's journey by sharing what has been particularly useful in their own ongoing recovery.

Taking inventory: Taking an honest look at one's character and actions to become aware of any damage or harm that one might have committed. This is a regular practice in recovery, particularly undertaken while working Steps Four and Ten.

The Twelve Steps and Twelve Traditions Book: An official AA publication that explains in depth the meaning and purpose of the Twelve Steps and Twelve Traditions. Also referred to as "The Twelve and Twelve" in abbreviated form. Other recovery programs such as Narcotics Anonymous, Overeaters Anonymous, and Adult Children of Anonymous have their own versions of this literature.

Working the Steps: A person's committed and conscious effort to engage each of the Twelve Steps in sequence and to apply the teachings and insights to their lives. Working the Steps is often done in consultation with a sponsor. Although the Steps are referenced at almost all Twelve-Step meetings, there are dedicated meetings where the Steps are the primary focus.

Resources

Adult Children of Alcoholics: www.adultchildren.org

Al-Anon/Alateen: www.al-anon.org

Alcoholics Anonymous: www.aa.org

Buddhist Recovery Network: www.buddhistrecovery.org

Co-Dependents Anonymous: www.coda.org

LifeRing: www.lifering.org

Narcotics Anonymous: www.na.org

Overeaters Anonymous: www.oa.org

Sexual and Love Addicts Anonymous: www.slaafws.org

SMART Recovery: www.smartrecovery.org

Unitarian Universalist Addictions Team: www.uua.org/care/ addictions

Unitarian Universalist Association: www.uua.org